NEW NOTES ON THE GERMAN ARMY

No. 1

ARMOURED AND MOTORIZED DIVISIONS

NOT TO BE PUBLISHED

The information given in this document is not to be communicated, either directly or indirectly, to the Press or any person not holding an official position in His Majesty's Service.

Prepared under the Direction of
The Chief of the Imperial General Staff.

THE WAR OFFICE,
6th *May*, 1942.

This Document must not fall into Enemy Hands

INTRODUCTION TO "NEW NOTES" SERIES

With this " Note " begins a new group of publications on the German army. So much information is now arriving covering all the theatres of the war that it is possible to assess within reasonably accurate limits the extent and value of changes in German organization and equipment as they occur. " Notes on the German Army—War—1940," aimed at providing a comprehensive handbook on the German army, but the changes which are constantly going on have caused large portions of that publication to be no longer accurate. In order to keep pace with alterations it is proposed to start a series of pamphlets which will amend the " Notes on the German Army—War—1940," and at the same time build up a new book of reference for intelligence officers. These pamphlets will be entitled " New Notes on the German Army."

As new material is bound to cut across a number of chapters in the " Notes on the German Army—War—1940," each of the " New Notes " will contain a list of paragraphs in the earlier publication which are superseded.

Ultimately, when a number of " New Notes " has been issued, it is intended to collate and re-issue them, including any new information which may then have come in, as " Notes on the German Army—1942." In the meantime, holders of the " Notes on the German Army—War," are advised to delete each superseded paragraph in that publication and insert references to the " New Notes " as these publications appear.

The " Periodical Notes on the German Army " will continue to be published. They will contain reports on operations together with tactical lessons and possible future tendencies. " Periodical Notes on the German Army," No. 39, which is being printed concurrently with the present " New Notes," deals with the tactical employment of artillery in armoured divisions.

DISTRIBUTION

All Arms	Scale A.
G.H.Q., Home Forces	10 copies
Command H.Q. (incl. A.A.)	5 ,,
London & Northern Ireland Districts	5 ,,
Corps H.Q. (incl. A.A.)	4 ,,
Divisional H.Q. (incl. A.A.)	3 ,,
Brigade H.Q. (incl. A.A.)	2 ,,
All Group H.Qs.	2 ,,
H.Q., Areas, Districts, Garrisons, Sub-Areas	1 copy
Intelligence Training Centre	150 copies
Intelligence Training Centre (Cambridge Wing)	50 ,,

CONTENTS

	PAGE
Introduction to " New Notes " series	ii of Cover
Preface	3
Introduction	4

PART I.—ORGANIZATION

A. Armoured division—

Composition of the armoured division	5
Mechanized reconnaissance unit	6
Tank regiment	7
Lorried infantry regiment	8
Motor cycle battalion	9
Artillery regiment	10
Anti-tank battalion	facing 10
Services	11
Repair and workshop units in an armoured division	12
Summary of personnel, A.F.Vs., and weapons in an armoured division	facing 16
Comparison between the British and the German armoured division	17

B. Motorized division—

	PAGE
Composition of the motorized division	18
Mechanized reconnaissance unit	18
Motorized infantry regiment	- 19
Motor cycle battalion	9
Artillery regiment	10
Anti-tank battalion	*facing* 10
Services	20
Repair and workshop units in a motorized division	20
Summary of personnel, armoured cars and weapons in a motorized division	*facing* 20
Allotment of repair services	*facing* 21
Comparison between British (normal) division and the German motorized division	21

C. G.H.Q. troops—

Assault artillery	22
Anti-tank battalion with guns on S.P. mountings	22
Motorized anti-aircraft battalion	23
Mixed anti-aircraft battery (G.A.F.)	24

PART II.—EQUIPMENT

Particulars of German tanks	*facing* 24
Particulars of French and Czech tanks	25
Particulars of German armoured cars	26
Machine carbine and machine gun	27
Anti-tank rifle, anti-tank guns, and tank guns	28
Mortars, infantry guns, and assault guns	30
Divisional artillery weapons	31
Anti-aircraft guns	32

PREFACE

The following paragraphs and appendices of "Notes on the German Army—War" are superseded by the present "New Notes."

  Chapter I, para. 8
      ,, 9
      ,, 13
      ,, 14
      ,, 15
  Chapter III ,, 3
      ,, 4
      ,, 6
      ,, 11
  Chapter IV ,, 3
  Chapter V ,, 4
      ,, 7
      ,, 8
  Chapter VI ,, 7
      ,, 8
      ,, 13 (organization of mixed battery)
  Chapter VII ,, 1 (c) (i)
      ,, 3
      ,, 5
      ,, 7
      ,, 9
    Appendix VIII
      XIII, Serials 15 and 26
      XV, Mixed battery
      XVI, Serials 1, 2, 13
      XVII
      XVIII
      XIX
      XX
      XXI
      XXII
      XXIII, Serials 5, 6
      XXIV, Serials 3, 4, 8

In addition, where statements made in Chapter XI of "Notes on the German Army—War" regarding the services of armoured and motorized divisions conflict with page 11 and page 20 of the present "New Notes," the latter should be taken as correct.

INTRODUCTION

"Notes on the German Army—War" give the organization of armoured and motorized divisions as it was at the time of the Battle of France. Since then considerable changes have been introduced in the organization of both these types of divisions.

Armoured divisions of normal type.—Despite the successes achieved in Poland and France by the former type of armoured division (which included 416 tanks organized in a tank brigade of two tank regiments, each of two battalions), it was clear by the time of the Balkan campaign that considerable changes in organization had been introduced. Details of these changes were obtained after the start of the Russian campaign. The German armoured division now has only one tank regiment, of three battalions, with 201 tanks. The 5·7-ton Pz. Kw. I tank has, however, been withdrawn, and the proportion of light medium tanks in the regiment is now much higher than formerly. The reduction in the number of tanks has also been accompanied by a very considerable increase both in the strength and fire power of the lorried infantry brigade, which now consists of two lorried infantry regiments and a motor cycle battalion. The artillery regiment of the armoured division now has a third (medium) battery. The fire-power of the armoured division as a whole has thus been increased.

Light armoured divisions.—Reports were received in the early months of 1941 about the formation of light armoured divisions. The only light armoured division identified was, however, the 5th Light (Colonial) Armoured Division, which appears to have been an experimental organization for North Africa, since after some months in Libya it was converted to an armoured division.

Heavy armoured divisions.—At the beginning of 1941 it appeared likely, in view of a number of reports received, that heavy armoured divisions equipped with tanks up to 90 tons in weight were being formed. No such armoured division has as yet been identified, and there is no confirmation of heavy tanks being produced, apart from the 31-ton French "Char B."

Motorized divisions.—The organization of motorized divisions has undergone two principal changes. The infantry establishment has been altered from three infantry regiments to two infantry regiments and a motor cyclist battalion, and the artillery regiment has been given a third (medium) battery.

PART I.—ORGANIZATION

A. ARMOURED DIVISION

COMPOSITION OF THE ARMOURED DIVISION

The armoured division consists of :—

	PAGE
H.Q.	
Mechanized reconnaissance unit...	6
*Divisional signals	—
Tank regiment	7
Lorried infantry brigade, consisting of two lorried infantry regiments and a motor cycle battalion ...	8 & 9
Artillery regiment	10
Anti-tank battalion	facing 10
†Engineer battalion	—
Services	11

In addition, when engaged in active operations, and particularly in the spearhead of the attack, an armoured division may have some of the following units from the G.H.Q. pool allotted to it :—

Assault artillery troops	22
‡Anti-tank battalion with guns on S.P. mountings ...	22
‡Motorized anti-aircraft battalion...	23
Mixed anti-aircraft battery (G.A.F.)	24

The table facing page 17 shows the organization of the armoured division in outline, and a summary of personnel, A.F.Vs., and weapons in an armoured division is given in the table facing page 16.

NOTES.

* As no substantial change has been reported in the organization of this unit, since the publication of " Notes on the German Army—War," it is omitted from the present " New Notes."

† Recent changes in the organization of this unit are given in summary form in the tables facing pp. 16 and 17. Full details will be published in subsequent " New Notes."

‡ These units may also be divided up and allotted to divisions by companies.

MECHANIZED RECONNAISSANCE UNIT

1. *Organization:*

```
                            H.Q. and Sig. Tp.
        ┌──────────────┬──────────┬──────────────┬──────────┐
    Armd. C. Sqn.   Armd. C. Sqn.           M.C. Rifle Sqn.  Hy. Sqn.
        │               │                       │
   ┌────┴────┐      ┌───┴────┐              (Hy. M.G. Tp.)
H.Q. and   4 Lt.   Hy. Tp.  Lt. Tp.    Lt. Tp.
Sig. Tp.  Armd. Cs. 6 Hy.   6 Lt.      8 Lt.
                   Armd. Cs. Armd. Cs. Armd. Cs.
```

Hy. Tp.: H.Q. — Sec. — Sec. Each 2 L.M.Gs.
Tp. H.Q.

Tp.: Sec. — Lt. Mortar Sec.
           1 Lt. 5-cm. (2-in.) mortar

Hy. M.G. Tp.: Tp. H.Q. — Sub-Sec. — Sub-Sec.
              Each 1 Hy. M.G.

Eng. Tp.: H.Q. — Close Support Tp. — A.Tk. Tp.
                 Two 7·5-cm.   Three 3·7-cm.
                 (2·95-in.) guns   (1·45-in.)
                                    A.Tk. guns.
                                    1 L.M.G.

Carries explosives, mines, bridging equipment, rubber boats, 3 L.M.Gs.

2. *Strength:* 27 Officers, 760 O.Rs.

3. *Fire-power:*

L.M.Gs.	72
Hy. M.Gs.	2
2-cm. (·79-in.) A.A./A.Tk. guns	20
5-cm. (2-in.) mortars	3
3·7-cm. (1·45-in.) A.Tk. guns	3
7·5-cm. (2·95-in.) inf. guns	2

Organization:

TANK REGIMENT

```
                                    H.Q.
    ┌───────────────┬────────┬────────┬──────────────────────┐
  H.Q. Sqn.         Bn.      Bn.      Bn.           Workshop Coy.
                                                    and Workshop Pl.
  ┌────┬─────────┬──────────┐
 Sig. Sec.  Lt. Tk. Tp.  5 Pz. Kw. II
 1 Pz. Kw. III
 2 Hy. A.C.V.
```

```
                                Bn.
  ┌──────────┬────────┬────────┬────────┬──────────┬────────┐
 H.Q.    H.Q. Sqn.  Pnr. Pl.  M.C. Pl.  A.A. Pl.  1 Lt. Sqn.  2 Lt. Sqn.  4 Med. Sqn
                   3 L.M.Gs.  4 L.M.Gs.  8 M.Gs.
```

H.Q. Sqn.
┌────┬─────────┬──────────┐
Sig. Sec. Lt. Tk. Tp. 5 Pz. Kw. II
1 Pz. Kw. III
2 Hy. A.C.V.

H.Q.   H.Q.
5 Pz. Kw. II   5 Pz. Kw. II
2 Pz. Kw. III   2 Pz. Kw. IV

Tp. — Each 5 Pz. Kw. III
Tp. — Each 4 Pz. Kw. IV

2. **Strength:** Approx. 2,650 all ranks.

3. **Tank establishment:** (First-line)

	Pz. Kw. II	Pz. Kw. III	Pz. Kw. IV	Total
Regt. H.Q. Sqn.	5	1	—	6
Bn. H.Q. Sqn.	5	1	—	6
Light Squadron	5	17	—	22
Medium Squadron	5	—	10	15
Total—Regiment	65	106	30	201

4. **Fire-power:**

L.M.Gs.	362
Hy. M.Gs.	24
2-cm. (·79-in.) A.A./A.Tk. guns	65
5-cm. (1·97-in.) guns	106
7·5-cm. (2·95-in.) guns	30

NOTE.—Every tank battalion is intended to have a reserve tank echelon of 6 tanks (2 Pz. Kw. II, 3 Pz. Kw. III, and 1 Pz. Kw. IV). Each tank battalion also has a light squadron (numbered 3, 7 or 11 as the case may be), which is a reserve and advanced training squadron. The total tank strength (including reserves) of the tank regiment is thus 285 tanks.

LORRIED INFANTRY REGIMENT

1. *Organization*:

```
                                        H.Q.
                                         |
          +------------------------------+------------------------------+
          |                                                             |
        H.Q. Coy.                                                      Bn.
          |                                                             |
   +------+------+------+                          +-------------+------+------+------+
   |      |      |      |                          |             |             |      |
 M.C. Pl. Pnr. Pl. Sig. Pl.                      Rifle Coy.   Rifle Coy.   Rifle Coy.  Heavy Coy.
 6 L.M.Gs. 3 L.M.Gs.                                                                      |
                                                                                          |
                                                                            +-------------+-------------+
                                                                            |                           |
                                                                       Inf. Gun Coy.                  Bn.
                                                                    Four 7·5-cm. (2·95-in.) Inf. guns
                                                                    Two 15-cm. (5·91-in.) Inf. guns
```

Rifle Coy.
- H.Q.
- Pl.
  - H.Q.
  - Sec. — Each 2 L.M.Gs.
- M.G. Pl.
  - H.Q.
  - Sec. — Each 2 Hy. M.Gs.
- Mortar Pl.
  - Sec.
  - Sec. — Each two 8·1-cm. (3·16-in.) mortars.

M.G. Coy.
- Pl.
  - Hy. M.G. Sec.
    - Sub. Sec.
    - Sub. Sec. — Each 1 Hy. M.G.
  - Lt. Mortar Sec.
    - Sec.
    - Sec. — 1 Lt. 5-cm. (2-in.) mortar.

Heavy Coy.
- A.Tk. Pl.
  - Three 3·7-cm. (1·45-in.) A.Tk. guns
  - 1 L.M.G.
- Lt. Inf. Gun Pl.
  - Two 7·5-cm. (2·95-in.) Inf. guns
  - Pnr. Pl.
  - 3 L.M.Gs.

Pl. H.Q. — 1 A.Tk. rifle

2. *Strength*: 71 Officers, 2,579 O.Rs.

3. *Fire-power*:

L.M.Gs.	125
Hy. M.Gs.	28
A.Tk. rifles	18
5-cm. (2-in.) mortars	18
8·1-cm. (3·16-in.) mortars	12
3·7-cm. (1·45-in.) A.Tk. guns	6
7·5-cm. (2·95-in.) Inf. guns	8
15-cm. (5·91-in.) Inf. guns	2

MOTOR CYCLE BATTALION

1. *Organization:*

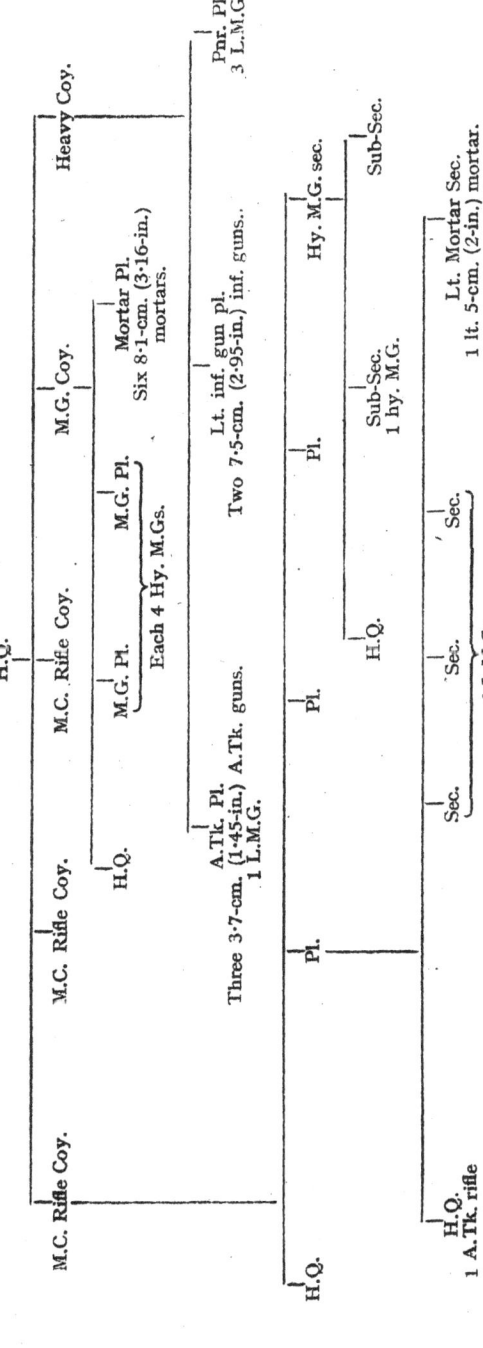

2. *Strength:* 27 Officers, 1,065 O.Rs.

3. *Fire-power:*
   L.M.Gs. 58
   Hy. M.Gs. 14
   A.Tk. rifles 9
   5-cm. (2-in.) mortars 9
   8·1-cm. (3·16-in.) mortars ... 6
   3·7-cm. (1·45-in.) A.Tk. guns ... 3
   7·5-cm. (2·95-in.) inf. guns ... 2

ARTILLERY REGIMENT

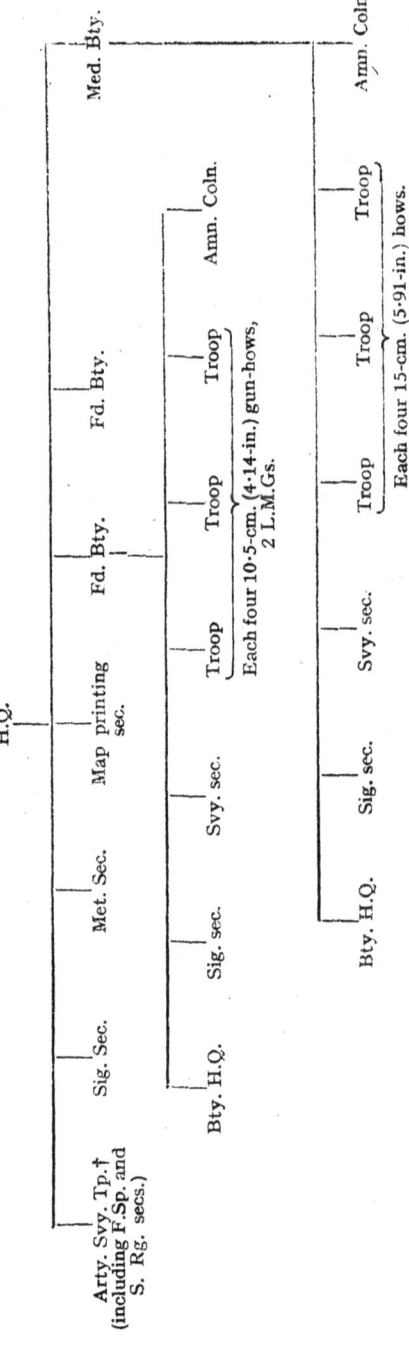

1. *Organisation:*

   H.Q.
   - Arty. Svy. Tp.† (including F.Sp. and S. Rg. secs.)
   - Sig. Sec.
   - Met. Sec.
   - Map printing sec.
   - Fd. Bty.
   - Fd. Bty.
   - Med. Bty.

   Fd. Bty.:
   - Bty. H.Q.
   - Sig. sec.
   - Svy. sec.
   - Troop
   - Troop
   - Troop
   - Amn. Coln.

   Each four 10·5-cm. (4·14-in.) gun-hows, 2 L.M.Gs.

   Med. Bty.:
   - Bty. H.Q.
   - Sig. sec.
   - Svy. sec.
   - Troop
   - Troop
   - Troop
   - Amn. Coln.

   Each four 15-cm. (5·91-in.) hows. 2 L.M.Gs.

   † Attached to artillery regiments of armoured, but not of motorized, divisions.

2. *Strength:* 79 officers, 1,969 O.Rs.

3. *Fire-power:*
   - 10·5-cm. (4·14-in.) gun/hows. 24
   - 15-cm. (5·91-in.) hows. 12
   - L.M.Gs. 18

[To face page 10

ANTI-TANK BATTALION

1. Organization:

```
Bn. Headquarters.
  Bn. Comd.
  Adj.
  Orderly Offr.
  Messing Offr.
  M.O.
  Asst. M.O.
  Technical Offr.
  5 lorries.
  4 M.Cs.

Signal section.
  Sig. Offr.
  6 Pack wireless sub-sections b.
  2 Lt. wireless sub-sections d.
  1 Telephone sub-section.
  10 lorries.
  2 M.Cs.
```

```
1 Company ── 2 Company ── 3 Company ── Transport

Coy. H.Q.
  Coy. Comd.
  C.S.M.
  4 motor cyclists.
  Orderly.
  1 office truck.

Pl. H.Q.                 Pl. H.Q.
  Pl. Cond.                (as for light platoon, but 2
  Sjt.                     tractors with trailers, 2 dri-
  4 motor cyclists.        vers)
  2 C.Rs.
  2 L.M.Gs.
  1 truck.
  1 tractor with trailer for amn.
  1 driver.

1 Platoon (light)    2 Platoon (med.)    3 Platoon (med.)

Sec. Sec.           Sec. Sec. Sec.      Sec. Sec. Sec.

3·7-cm. (1·45-in.) gun,    5-cm. (1·97-in.) gun, crew
each a crew of 4 men.      of 7 men.

Transport
  A. Echelon.
    3 personnel lorries.
    1 field kitchen.
    1 P.O.L. lorry.
    1 workshop lorry.
    2 medical lorries.
    1 supply lorry.
    1 M.C.
  B. Echelon.
    1 baggage lorry.
    1 personnel lorry.
    2 supply lorries.
    2 M.Cs.

Coy. Transport.
  1 personnel lorry.
  Baggage lorry.
  Workshop lorry.
  Ammunition lorry.
  Field kitchen.
  Supply lorry.
  1 P.O.L. lorry.
  1 P.O.L. and equip-
    ment lorry.
  2 M.Cs.

M.T. Repair Section.
  4 lorries.
  1 M.C.
```

2. Strength (*approx.*):—21 officers, 578 O.Rs.

3. Fire-power:—3·7-cm. (1·45-in.) A.Tk. guns 12
    5-cm. (1·97-in.) A.Tk. guns 18
    L.M.Gs. 18

4. Transport (*approx.*):—Motor cycles 64
    Tractors 44
    Other M.T. vehicles ... 68

SERVICES

The services of an armoured division include the following :—

1. *Divisional supply unit*, under Div. Supply Comd. (*Divisions-Nachschubführer*) :

H.Q.	6 officers	55 O.Rs.
Mot. supply coy.	4 ,,	190 ,,
3 mot. workshop coys., each	1 officer	112 ,,
9 light supply colns., each	1 ,,	30 ,,
6 hy. ,, ,, ,,	1 ,,	63 ,,
Total	28 officers,	1,229 O.Rs.

The hy. supply colns. are mainly for P.O.L., but some may be used for the transport of amn., e.g. one div. in Russia employed 4½ hy. colns. for P.O.L. and 1½ for amn.

2. *Divisional rations supply* (*Divisions-Intendant*) :

Rations office (*Verpflegungsamt*)	—	29 O.Rs.
Mot. bakery coy.	2 officers	140 ,,
Mot. butcher coy.	1 officer	50 ,,
Div. pay office	—	2 ,,
Total	3 officers	221 O.Rs.

3. *Divisional medical unit* :

2 mot. medical coys., eac	8 officers	262 O.Rs.
3 M.T. ambulance sections, each	1 officer	40 ,,
Total	19 officers,	644 O.Rs.

The division may also have attached to it a motorized field hospital of 6 officers and 70 O.Rs.

4. *Field post office* ... 18 officials.

5. *Military police section*, of 1 officer and 36 O.Rs.

Total ... 51 officers, 2,148 O.Rs.

REPAIR AND WORKSHOP UNITS IN ARMOURED DIVISIONS

I. Establishments and Allotment

1. *Tank regiment*
    i. Every tank squadron has a repair section " a ", with the following establishments :—

    (a) *Personnel*
    - 1 N.C.O. (tank fitter) section leader.
    - 3 N.C.Os. (tank fitters).
    - 13 tank fitters.
    - 2 tank fitters (W/T).
    - 1 armourer's assistant.
    - 4 drivers.
       Total : 4 N.C.Os. and 20 men.

    (b) *M.T.*
    - 4 motor vehicles.
    - 3 M.C. combinations.

    ii. Each tank battalion H.Q. and tank regiment H.Q. has a repair section " b", with the following establishment :—

    (a) *Personnel*
    - 1 N.C.O. (tank fitter) section leader
    - 3 tank fitters (for tank regt. H.Q.)

    or 5 tank fitters (for tank bn. H.Q.)

    - 1 motor cyclist (tank fitter, W/T)
    - 1 car driver (tank fitter, W/T)
    - 1 lorry driver.
       Total for tank regt. H.Q. : 1 N.C.O. and 6 men.
       Total for tank bn. H.Q. : 1 N.C.O. and 8 men.

    (b) *M.T.*
    - 2 motor vehicles.
    - 1 M.C. combination.

iii. The tank regiment has an armoured workshop company and an additional armoured workshop platoon. The establishment of an armoured workshop company and platoon is :—

	Offrs.	O.Rs.	Motor Vehicles (Trailers)	M.C. Combinations
Armd. workshop coy. ..	4	198	52 (9)	10
Armd. workshop platoon	NOT KNOWN			

The organization is as follows :—

Armd. workshop company :
  H.Q.
  1 Platoon.
  2 Platoon.
  Recovery platoon.
  Armoury.
  Signals workshop.
  Transport.

Armd. workshop platoon :
  H.Q.
  Platoon.
  Armoury.

iv. The divisional services include three mechanized workshop companies, possibly grouped together as a workshop unit. The pre-war organization of a mechanized workshop company was :—
  H.Q.
  1 Platoon (M.T. workshop platoon).
  2 Platoon (M.T. ,, ,,).
  3 Platoon (armoury).
  Transport.

Its strength was as follows :—
(a) *Personnel*
    Officers 1.
    O.Rs.   101.

(b) *M.T.*
    Motor vehicles 21.
    Motor cycles 6.

2. Other units in the armoured division

  i. *Establishments*

    The establishments of repair services for other units in the armoured division are as follows :—

  (a) *Repair sub-sections.*

Repair sub-section " a " :

1 M.T. corporal (in side-car), sub-section leader.
1 M.C. driver (engine fitter).
1 engine fitter.
1 car driver (engine fitter).
    1 heavy M.C. with side-car.
    1 small repair car.

Repair sub-section " b " :

1 M.T. corporal (in side-car), sub-section leader.
1 M.C. driver (engine fitter).
6 engine fitters or tank fitters.
1 electrical mechanic (spare fitter).
2 drivers (one car, one lorry) (engine fitters).
    1 heavy M.C. with side-car.
    2 motor vehicles.

Repair sub-section " c " :

1 M.T. corporal (in side-car), sub-section leader.
1 corporal (tank fitter)
1 M.C. driver.
12 tank fitters (of whom 6 are engine fitters).
1 electrical mechanic (on M.C. combination).
2 signals mechanics (drivers' mates).
1 car driver (engine fitter).
2 lorry drivers.
    2 heavy M.Cs. with side-cars.
    3 motor vehicles.

(b) *Repair detachments.*

Detachment " a " :

1 workshop master (official, middle grade).

1 corporal master fitter and engine fitter.

(x) 2 engine fitters (spare drivers).

1 engine fitter for M.Cs.

1 smith and welder.

1 M.C. driver (on M.C. combination) (i/c equipment and clerk).

(y) 4 drivers (2 car and 2 lorry) (of whom 1 electrician and 1 engine fitter).

1 heavy M.C. with side-car.

4 motor vehicles.

Detachment " b " :

As for detachment " a ", except for item (x) which reads :—

(x) 3 engine fitters (spare drivers).

Detachment " c " :

As for detachment " a ", except for items (x) and (y) and an additional item (z) :—

(x) 5 engine fitters or tank fitters (of whom 3 spare drivers).

(y) 5 M.T. drivers (2 car and 3 lorry) (of whom 1 electrician, 1 welder's assistant and 1 engine driver).

(z) 1 medium cross-country lorry, open, for tyres.

ii. *Allotment*

For the allotment of repair services to other units of the armoured division, *see* the table facing page 17.

II. Employment

1. As a rough guide to the scales of repairs which can be undertaken by repair units, etc., the following may be used :—

Repair units—repairs on a vehicle taking up to four working hours.

Workshop units—repairs on a vehicle taking up to 12 working hours.

Army M.T. park—repairs on a vehicle taking up to 24 working hours.

Repair units are forbidden to do welding in armour on gashes more than 10 cm. (approximately 4 in.) long.

2. A workshop company has power tools, its own power and light, apparatus for oxyacetylene and electric welding, and a crane. Existing facilities on the spot (factories, etc.) are always used whenever possible. The workshop company may be some 12–18 miles behind the fighting tanks. It is, if convenient, split up into separate platoons.

3. i. *On the march.*

The repair sections travel with the " A " echelon (fighting vehicles). Part may be attached to the " B " echelon (battle transport) if necessary.

If a vehicle breaks down on the march the repair section leader decides whether the breakdown can be remedied by the repair section. In the meantime the rearmost vehicle of the repair section has stayed behind. In accordance with the decision of the repair section leader either the repair work is started immediately, or the vehicle is handed over to the commander of the recovery platoon to be towed away.

In this way one vehicle after another stays behind, at first mostly the motor-cycles, then, according to the seriousness of the damage, a semi-tracked vehicle.

ii. *In battle.*

In battle the repair sections are under the orders of the battalion commander. As a rule they follow behind the fighting troops in their battalion sector and are commanded by the battalion technical officer (M.T.). They go over the area looking for broken down vehicles. Every effort is made to get repairs done as soon as possible so that the maximum number of vehicles is kept in the battle.

4. Very great importance is attached by the Germans to the immediate recovery of vehicles. Not merely is the recovery of German vehicles very efficient, but also units will often send out detachments to " recover " enemy M.T. For instance, a tank battalion may send out a detachment of an officer, one or two N.C.Os. and six or eight men, transported in one or two cross-country vehicles and protected by one or two light tanks.

[To face page 16

ARMOURED DIVISION—SUMMARY OF PERSONNEL, A.F.Vs., WEAPONS AND M.T.

Unit	Personnel	Tanks			Armoured cars		Small arms			A.A. and/or A.Tk. guns			Mortars		Close support artillery		Divisional artillery		M.T.	
		Pz. Kw. IV	Pz. Kw. III	Pz. Kw. II	Heavy Armd. cars	Lt. Armd. cars	L.M.Gs.	Hy. M.Gs.	A.Tk. Rifles	2-cm. (·79-in.) A.A. & A.Tk. guns	3·7-cm. (1·45-in.) A.Tk. guns	5-cm. (1·97-in.) A.Tk. guns	5-cm. (2-in.) mortars	8·1-cm. (3·16-in.) mortars	7·5-cm. (2·95-in.) inf. guns	15-cm. (5·91-in.) inf. guns	10·5-cm. (4·14 in.) gun-hows	15-cm. (5·91-in.) hows	M.Vs.	M.Cs.
(1)	(2)	(3)	(4)	(5)	(6)	(7)	(8)	(9)	(10)	(11)	(12)	(13)	(14)	(15)	(16)	(17)	(18)	(19)		
Div. H.Q.	185	—	—	—	—	—	—	2	—	—	—	—	—	—	—	—	—	—	31	39
Recce. unit	787	—	—	—	12	36	72	2	—	20	3	—	3	—	2	—	—	—	117	131
Div. sigs. bn.	422	—	—	—	—	—	17	—	—	—	—	—	—	—	—	—	—	—	102	27
Tank regt.	2,650	30	106	65	—	—	362	24	—	65	—	106	—	—	30	—	—	—	453	190
A.Tk. bn.	599	—	—	—	—	—	18	—	—	—	12	18	—	—	—	—	—	—	112	64
Lorried inf. bde.	6,434	—	—	—	—	—	308	70	45	—	15	—	45	30	18	4	—	—	1,070	710
Div. arty. regt.	2,048	—	—	—	—	—	18	—	—	—	—	—	—	—	—	—	24	12	420	160
Arty. svy. tp.	267	—	—	—	—	—	—	—	—	—	—	—	—	—	—	—	—	—	—	—
Engineer bn.	875	—	—	—	—	—	37	—	—	1	—	—	—	—	—	—	—	—	139	33
Services	2,199	—	—	—	—	—	—	—	—	—	—	—	—	—	—	—	—	—	481	124
First line reinforcements bn.	875	—	—	—	—	—	—	—	—	—	—	—	—	—	—	—	—	—	—	—
Total	17,341	30	106 / 201	65	12 / 48	36	832	98	45	86	30	124	48	30	50	4	24	12	2,925	1,478

NOTE.—*Engineer battalion.*—The third (armoured) company has the following special transport:—11 Pz.Kw. I, 1 Pz.Kw. II and possibly some heavier tanks for bridge-laying.

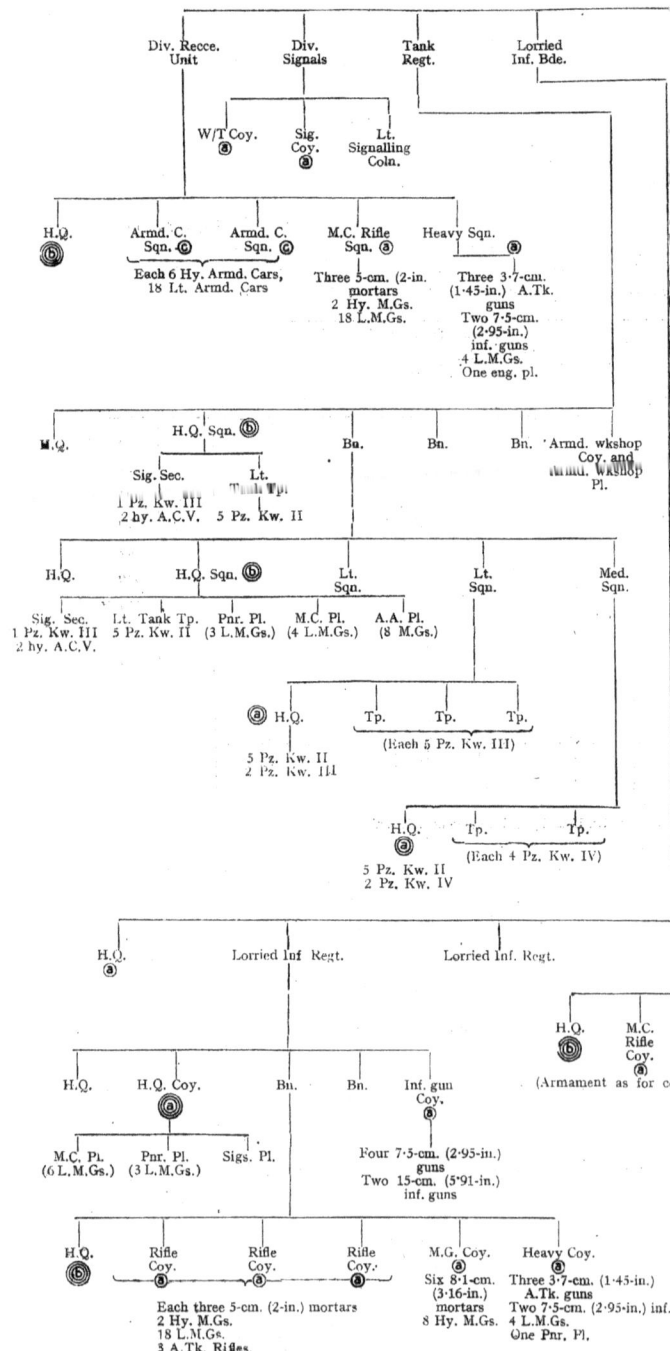

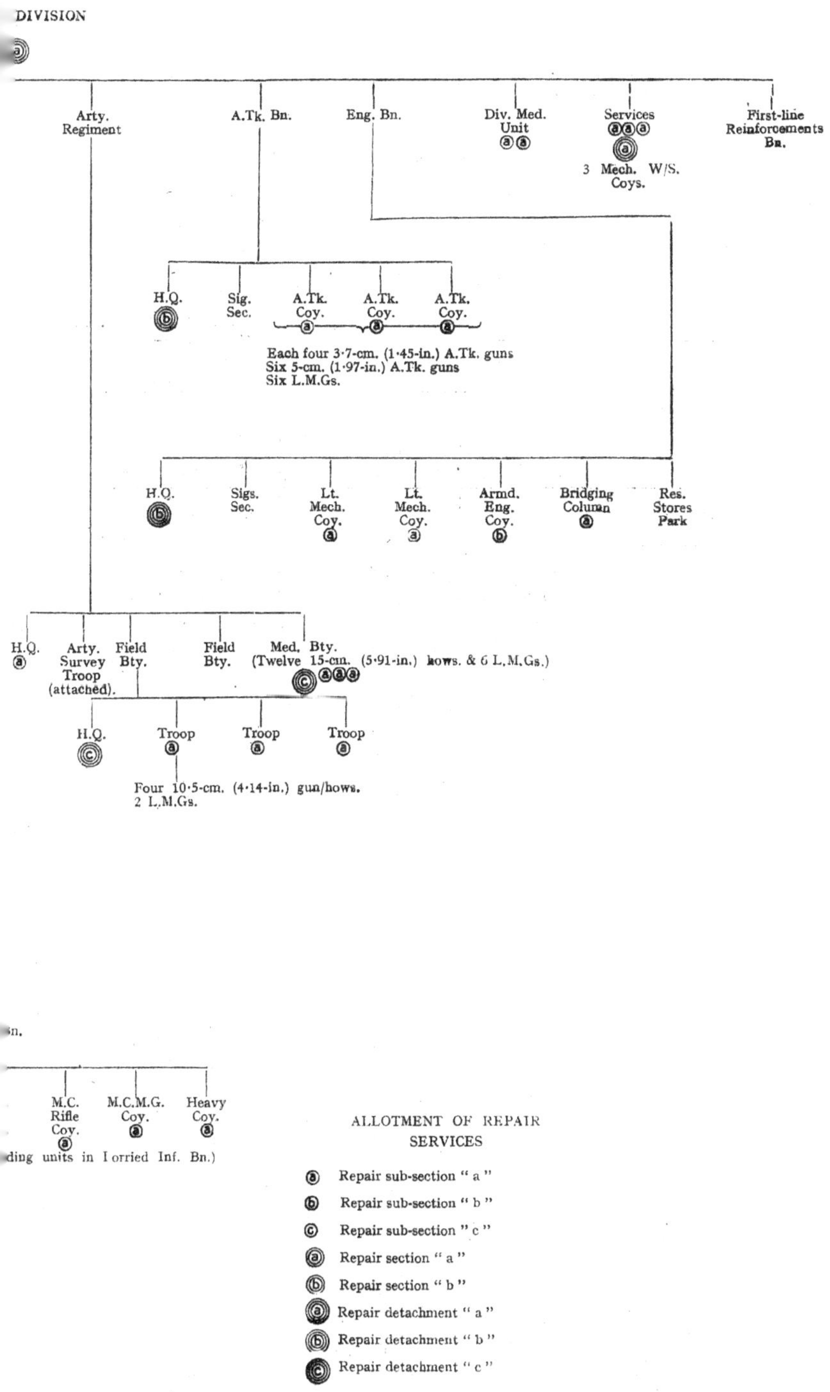

DIVISION

```
         |               |             |            |              |                    |
       Arty.          A.Tk. Bn.     Eng. Bn.    Div. Med.       Services         First-line
     Regiment                                     Unit           ⓐⓐⓐ          Reinforcements
                                                  ⓐⓑ              ⓒ                  Bn.
                                                             3 Mech. W/S.
                                                                Coys.
```

```
   |        |         |         |         |
  H.Q.    Sig.     A.Tk.     A.Tk.     A.Tk.
   ⓑ     Sec.     Coy.      Coy.      Coy.
                    ⓐ        ⓐ         ⓐ
                Each four 3·7-cm. (1·45-in.) A.Tk. guns
                Six 5-cm. (1·97-in.) A.Tk. guns
                Six L.M.Gs.
```

```
   |       |        |        |         |          |           |
  H.Q.   Sigs.    Lt.      Lt.      Armd.     Bridging      Res.
   ⓑ    Sec.    Mech.    Mech.     Eng.      Column       Stores
               Coy.     Coy.      Coy.         ⓐ           Park
                ⓐ       ⓐ         ⓑ
```

```
   |        |         |          |
  H.Q.    Arty.    Field      Field       Med. Bty.
   ⓐ    Survey    Bty.       Bty.     (Twelve 15-cm. (5·91-in.) hows. & 6 L.M.Gs.)
         Troop                                   ⓒⓐⓐⓐ
        (attached).
```

```
          |         |          |         |
        H.Q.     Troop      Troop     Troop
         ⓒ        ⓐ          ⓐ         ⓐ
              Four 10·5-cm. (4·14-in.) gun/hows.
              2 L.M.Gs.
```

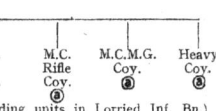

```
   |          |          |
  M.C.     M.C.M.G.    Heavy
  Rifle     Coy.       Coy.
  Coy.       ⓐ          ⓐ
   ⓐ
 ding units in lorried Inf. Bn.)
```

ALLOTMENT OF REPAIR SERVICES

- ⓐ   Repair sub-section "a"
- ⓑ   Repair sub-section "b"
- ⓒ   Repair sub-section "c"
- ⓐ   Repair section "a"
- ⓑ   Repair section "b"
- ⓐ   Repair detachment "a"
- ⓑ   Repair detachment "b"
- ⓒ   Repair detachment "c"

COMPARISON BETWEEN THE BRITISH AND GERMAN ARMOURED DIVISION

(For the organization of the British armoured division, *see* the Field Service Pocket Book.)

1. *Reconnaissance.*—The German reconnaissance unit conforms to the German plan of having in units of this type a scouting element (the two armoured car squadrons), a holding element (the M.C. rifle squadron), and a support element (the heavy squadron). On the new British establishment each troop in the armoured car regiment has a scouting element (two armoured cars and two scout cars) and a holding element (two "blitzbugs" and two M.Cs.), but there is no support element within the regiment.

2. *Tanks* (striking element).—The British division has a larger number of tanks than the German (340 tanks as against 201).

3. *Infantry* (holding element).—The German division has four battalions of lorried infantry and a M.C. battalion as compared with two motor battalions and a lorried infantry battalion in the British. In the German division, also, the holding element is grouped together under the lorried infantry brigade H.Q., while in the British it is divided between the armoured brigades and the support group.

4. *Support element.*—In the German division the artillery regiment, the anti-tank battalion, and the Mot. A.A. bn. (when attached) are all divisional troops. In the British division the artillery regiment, the anti-tank regiment and the light A.A. regiment are placed (along with the lorried infantry battalion) under command of a support group H.Q. The British organization is, however, fully as flexible as the German, since the units forming the support group may either be employed as a group (e.g. to hold a line) or sub-allotted to the armoured brigade.

5. *Artillery.*—The British division has 24 field guns, the German 24 field and 12 medium guns, and also 24 close support guns. (Great reliance is also placed by the Germans on support from bombers and dive-bombers for divisions in the spearhead of the attack.)

6. *Anti-tank guns.*—The German anti-tank battalion has 30 guns, and there are a number of anti-tank guns in other units of the German division. In consequence, the German division has a larger number of anti-tank guns than the British, and many of the German guns are of greater calibre than the British.

B.—MOTORIZED DIVISION

COMPOSITION OF THE MOTORIZED DIVISION

A motorized division consists of :—

	PAGE
H.Q.	—
Mechanized reconnaissance unit	18
*Divisional signals	—
Two motorized regiments	19
Motor-cycle battalion	9
Artillery regiment	10
Anti-tank battalion	facing 10
*Engineer battalion	—
Services	20

In addition, when engaged in active operations, and particularly in the spearhead of the attack, a motorized division may have some of the following units from the G.H.Q. pool allotted to it :—

	PAGE
Assault artillery troops	22
†Anti-tank battalion with guns on S.P. mountings	22
†Motorized anti-aircraft battalion	23
Mixed anti-aircraft battery (G.A.F.)	24

The table facing page 21 shows the organization of the motorized division in outline, and a summary of personnel, armoured cars and weapons in a motorized division is given in the table facing page 20.

NOTES

* As no substantial change has been reported in the organization and equipment of these units since the publication of " Notes on the German Army—War," they are omitted from the present "New Notes."
† These units may also be divided up and allotted to divisions by companies.

MECHANIZED RECONNAISSANCE UNIT

1. *Organization*

The mechanized reconnaissance unit in a motorized division is organized in the same way as that in the armoured division, except that the former has only one armoured car squadron.

2. *Strength :*
   22 officers, 622 O.Rs.

3. *Fire-power :*

L.M.Gs.	47
Hy. M.Gs.	2
2-cm. (·79-in.) A.A./A.Tk. guns	10
5-cm. (2-in.) mortars	3
3·7-cm. (1·45-in.) A.Tk. guns	3
7·5-cm. (2·95-in.) inf. guns	2

MOTORIZED INFANTRY REGIMENT

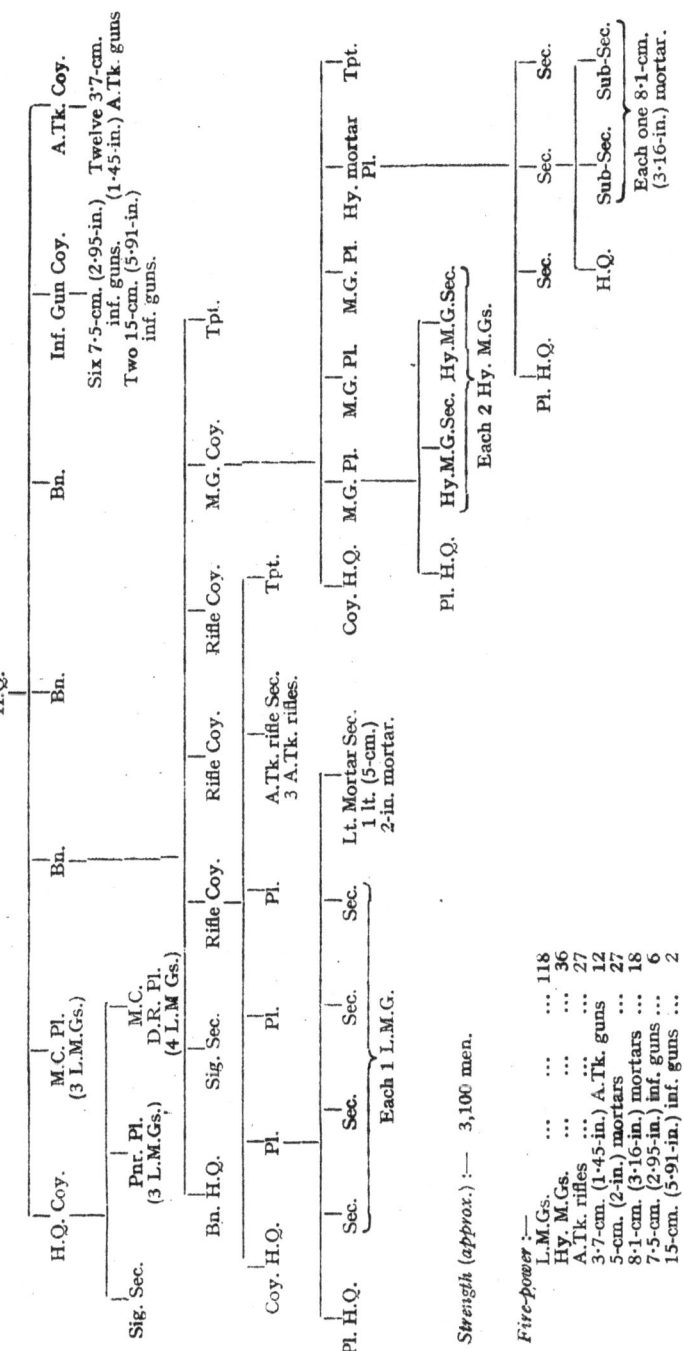

2. *Strength (approx.)*:— 3,100 men.

3. *Fire-power*:—
   L.M.Gs. 118
   Hy. M.Gs. 36
   A.Tk. rifles 27
   3·7-cm. (1·45-in.) A.Tk. guns 12
   5-cm. (2-in.) mortars ... 27
   8·1-cm. (3·16-in.) mortars ... 18
   7·5-cm. (2·95-in.) inf. guns ... 6
   15-cm. (5·91-in.) inf. guns ... 2

SERVICES

The services of a motorized division include the following :—

1. *Divisional supply unit*, under Div. Supply Comd. (*Divisions-Nachschubführer*) :

H.Q.	6 officers	55 O.Rs.
Mot. supply coy.	4 ,,	190 ,,
2 mot. workshop coys., each	1 ,,	112 ,,
8 lt. supply colns., each	1 ,,	30 ,,
2 hy. supply colns. for P.O.L., each	1 ,,	63 ,,
Total	22 officers	835 O.Rs.

2. *Divisional rations supply* (*Divisions-Intendant*) :

Rations office (*Verpflegungsamt*)	—	22 O.Rs.
Mot. bakery coy.	2 officers	140 ,,
Mot. butcher coy.	1 officer	50 ,,
Div. Pay Office	—	2 ,,
Total	3 officers	221 O.Rs.

3. *Divisional medical unit* :

2 mot. medical coys., each	8 officers	262 O.Rs.
3 M.T. ambulance sections, each	1 ,,	40 ,,
1 mot. field hospital	6 ,,	70 ,,
Total	25 officers	714 O.Rs.

4. *Field post office* ... 18 officials.

5. *Military police section*, of 1 officer and 36 O.Rs.

Total ... 51 officers 1,824 O.Rs.

REPAIR AND WORKSHOP UNITS IN MOTORIZED DIVISIONS

1. *Establishments*

The establishments of repair services for units of a motorized division are the same as those for units, other than the tank regiment, of the armoured division (*see* page 14).

2. *Allotment*

For the allotment of repair services to units of the motorized division, *see* the table facing page 21.

3. *Employment*

Repair services in a motorized division are employed on the same principles as those in the armoured division (*see* page 15).

MOTORIZED DIVISION—SUMMARY OF PERSONNEL, ARMOURED CARS, WEAPONS AND M.T.

Unit	Personnel	Armoured Cars		Small Arms			A.A. and/or A.Tk. guns			Mortars		Close support artillery		Divisional artillery		M.T.	
		Hy. Armd. cars	Lt. Armd. cars	L.M.Gs.	Hy. M.G.	A.Tk. Rifles	2-cm. (·79-in.) A.A. & A.Tk. guns	3·7-cm. (1·45-in.) guns	5-cm. (1·97-in.) A.Tk. guns	5-cm. (2-in.) mortars	8·1-cm. (3·16-in.) mortars	7·5-cm. (2·95-in.) inf. guns	15-cm. (5·91-in.) inf. guns	10·5-cm. (4·14-in.) gun-hows.	15-cm. (5·91-in.) hows.	M.Vs.	M.Cs.
(1)	(2)	(3)	(4)	(5)	(6)	(7)	(8)	(9)	(10)	(11)	(12)	(13)	(14)	(15)	(16)		
Div. H.Q.	185	—	—	—	2	—	—	—	—	—	—	—	—	—	—	30	39
Div. sig. bn.	422	—	—	17	—	—	—	—	—	—	—	—	—	—	—	102	27
Recce. unit	644	6	18	47	2	—	10	3	—	—	—	2	—	—	—	82	115
Two mot. inf. regts.	6,200	—	—	236	72	54	—	24	—	3	36	12	4	—	—	870	510
M.C. bn.	1,092	—	—	58	14	9	—	3	—	9	6	2	—	—	—	80	275
Arty. regt.	2,048	—	—	18	—	—	—	—	—	—	—	—	—	24	12	400	150
A.Tk. bn.	599	—	—	18	—	—	—	12	18	—	—	—	—	—	—	112	64
Eng. bn.	685	—	—	28	—	—	—	—	—	—	—	—	—	—	—	156	33
Services	1,875	—	—	—	—	—	—	—	—	—	—	—	—	—	—	375	63
First line reinforcements bn.	875	—	—	—	—	—	—	—	—	—	—	—	—	—	—	—	—
Totals	14,625	6	18	422	90	63	10	42	18	66	42	16	4	24	12	2,207	1,276

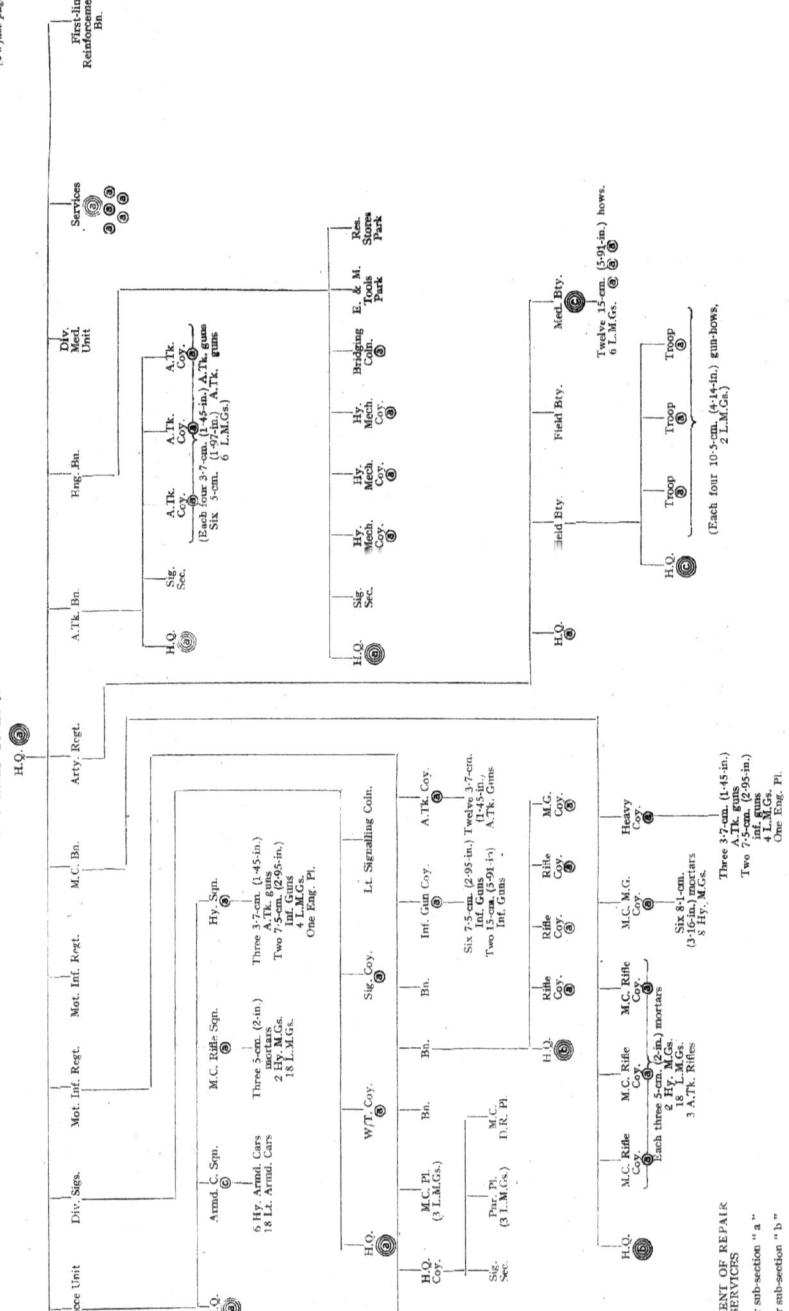

COMPARISON BETWEEN THE BRITISH (NORMAL) DIVISION AND THE GERMAN MOTORIZED DIVISION

(For the organization of the British division, see the Field Service Pocket Book.)

NOTE.—The structure of the British division resembles more closely that of the German infantry division than that of the German motorized division. As, however, the German infantry division is still mainly on a horsed basis, it is outside the scope of the present " New Notes ". It is thought, however, that the following comparison between the British (normal) division and the German motorized division may be instructive.

1. *Reconnaissance.*—As in the armoured division, the reconnaissance unit of the German motorized division includes a scouting element (one armoured car squadron), a holding element (M.C. rifle squadron) and a support element (the heavy squadron). In the British divisional reconnaissance battalion, each company includes a scouting and a holding element, and there is no support element on the German pattern.

2. *Infantry.*—The German division is weaker in infantry since it includes only two regiments (which correspond to British brigades) and an M.C. battalion. The German regiment, however, includes, besides three infantry battalions, an infantry gun company and an anti-tank company. Infantry weapons are also decentralized further in the German than in the British organization, since each German battalion has a machine-gun company, which also includes mortars.

3. *Artillery.*—The German division is weaker than the British in artillery since the German has only 24 field and 12 medium guns as compared with 72 field (and often 16 medium guns attached) in the British division. The German division has, however, 40 close support infantry guns distributed between the infantry regiments, the M.C. battalion, and the reconnaissance unit. It must also be remembered that in all campaigns of the present war the Germans have relied very considerably on bomber and dive-bomber support to offset the deficiency in divisional artillery.

4. *Engineers.*—The engineer battalion in the Germa motorized division, like the corresponding unit in the armoure division, includes a bridging column with sufficient equipmen to build a 60-yard bridge to take the 22-ton Pz. Kw. IV tank **The allotment of bridging** equipment to British divisiona engineers is smaller.

5. *Anti-tank guns.*—The German anti-tank battalion ha only 30 guns, but the anti-tank guns with other units of th division bring the divisional total up to a figure rather highe than the British total.

C.—G.H.Q. TROOPS

ASSAULT ARTILLERY

Assault artillery (7·5-cm. (2·95-in.) guns on Pz.Kw. II chassis) is organized in batteries of independent troops in th G.H.Q. pool. A battery consists of three troops, each c **six guns.**

The organization of units equipped with 15-cm. (5·91-in assault guns is not known.

ANTI-TANK BATTALION
(equipped with A.Tk. guns on S.P. mountings).

1. *Organization*

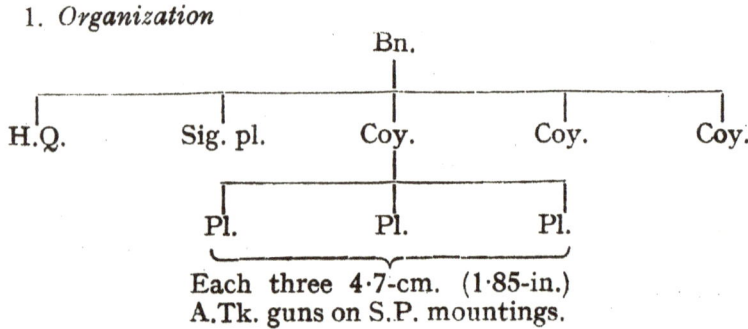

Each three 4·7-cm. (1·85-in.) A.Tk. guns on S.P. mountings.

2. *Fire-power*

    4·7-cm. (1·85-in.) A.Tk. guns 27

MOTORIZED ANTI-AIRCRAFT BATTALION

Motorized A.A. battalions consist of three (or, in some cases, six) companies, equipped with the following weapons :—

    3·7-cm. (1·45-in.) A.A. guns.
    2-cm. (·79-in.) A.A./A.Tk. guns.
    M.Gs.

The number of guns of each of the above types in a battalion may vary. Some battalions, however, are known to be equipped with twenty-four 2-cm. (·79-in.) A.A./A.Tk. guns, nine 3·7-cm. (1·45-in.) A.A. guns and 8 M.Gs. Some battalions also are equipped with guns on S.P. mountings.

MIXED ANTI-AIRCRAFT BATTERY (G.A.F.)

1. *Organization* :

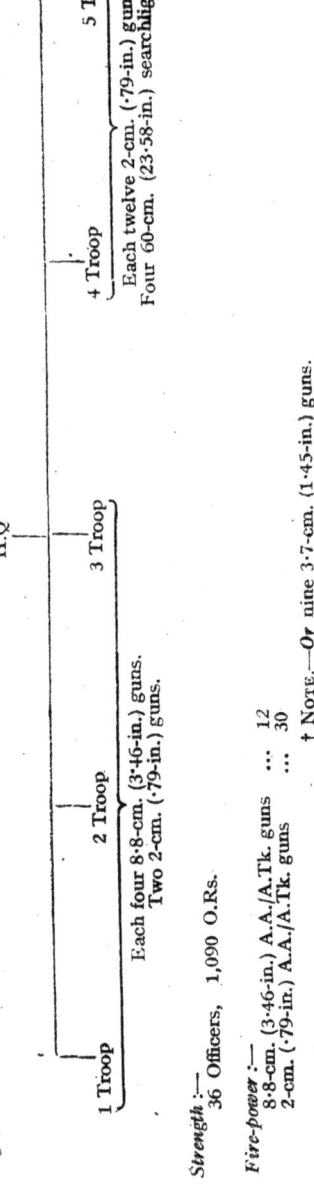

```
                              H.Q
    ┌──────────┬──────────┬──────────┬──────────┐
  1 Troop   2 Troop   3 Troop   4 Troop   5 Troop
```

1 Troop, 2 Troop, 3 Troop: Each four 8·8-cm. (3·46-in.) guns. Two 2-cm. (·79-in.) guns.

4 Troop, 5 Troop: Each twelve 2-cm. (·79-in.) guns.† Four 60-cm. (23·58-in.) searchlights.

2. *Strength* :—
   36 Officers, 1,090 O.Rs.

3. *Fire-power* :—
   8·8-cm. (3·46-in.) A.A./A.Tk. guns ... 12
   2-cm. (·79-in.) A.A./A.Tk. guns ... 30

† NOTE.—*Or* nine 3·7-cm. (1·45-in.) guns.

[To face page 24]

PART II.—EQUIPMENT
PARTICULARS OF GERMAN TANKS

(1)	Pz Kw I (2)	Pz Kw II (3)	Pz Kw III (4)	Pz Kw IV (5)
Weight	5-7 tons	9 tons	18/20 tons	22 tons
Crew	2	3	5	5
Dimensions. 1. Length 2. Width 3. Height 4. Belly clearance	12 ft. 6 in. 8 ft. 0 in. 5 ft. 7 in. 1 ft. to 1 ft. 6 in.	15 ft. 4 in. 7 ft. 2 in. 6 ft. 5 in. 0 ft. 11 in.	17 ft. 8 in. 9 ft. 9 in. 7 ft. 9 in. 0 ft. 9 in. to 1 ft. 0 in.	19 ft. 2 in. 9 ft. 5 in. 8 ft. 7 in. 1 ft. 2 in.
Armour. 1. Front	18 mm. (·708-in.)	20 mm. plus 20 mm. extra on gun mounting and front of superstructure; total 1·574 in.	50 mm. (1·968-in.).	30 mm. plus 30 mm. extra on front of driver and auxiliary gunner's compartment; total 2·362 in.
2. Sides	14 mm. (·551-in.)	18 mm. (·708-in.)	27 mm. (1·259-in.)	Turret sides and cupola 20 mm. (·787 in.). Sides of hull and superstructure 40 mm. (1·574-in.)
3. Top	14 mm. (·551-in.)	15 mm. ? (·590-in.)	27 mm. (top engine compartment). (1·063 in.)	Top of engine compartment 10 mm. (·393-in.)
Armament	2 M.Gs. co-axial	1 2-cm. (·79-in.) 1 M.G. } Co-axial	1 5-cm. gun (1·97-in.) 1 M.G. 1 M.G. hull } Co-axial	1 7·5-cm. (2·95-in.) Q.F. gun 1 M.G. 1 M.G. hull } Co-axial
Engine	Petrol	Petrol 6-cyl. Maybach	320 H.P. V-12. Petrol, water cooled.	320 H.P. V-12. Petrol. Water cooled.
Drive	Front	Front	Front	Front
Speed (max.)	32 m.p.h.	25 m.p.h.		25 m.p.h.
Communication	W/T	W/T and internal telephone system.	W/T	W/T
Performance 1. Trench crossing 2. Step 3. Water forded 4. Max. gradient	Estimated 4 ft. 7 in. 1 ft. 2 in. 2 ft. 0 in. 45°	Estimated 4 ft. 11 in. 1 ft. 11 in. 2 ft. 6 in. 45°	Estimated 5 ft. 7 in. 2 ft. 0 in. 2 ft. 11 in. —	Estimated 9 ft. 0 in. 2 ft. 3 in. 3 ft. 6 in.
Suspension	5 Bogie wheels. 1 Independently sprung, 4 connected by girder	5 independently sprung bogies on semi-elliptic leaf springs. Diameter of bogie wheels 22 in.	6 independent bogie wheels on rocker arms. Diameter of bogie wheels 20 in.	8 small bogie wheels in pairs, cantilever sprung to hull.
Remarks	May be used as Commander's tank with a square fixed turret.		Range : 100 miles (estimated).	Range : 100 miles (estimated).

PARTICULARS OF CZECH AND FRENCH TANKS

Czech and French tanks* (1)	CZECH			FRENCH		
	R.1 and S.1 light tanks (2)	L.T.35 S.IIA light tank (Pz.Kw. 35 t) (3)	L.T.H. light tank (Pz.Kw. 38 t) (4)	Hotchkiss H.39 light tank (5)	Somua S.40 medium tank (6)	Char B heavy tank (7)
Weight—tons	3·5-4	10·3	9·5	12	20	31
Crew	2	4	4	2	3	4
Dimensions:						
Length	10 ft. 3 in. and 8 ft. 6 in.	14 ft. 11 in.	16 ft. 1 in.	14 ft. 11 in.	18 ft. 7 in.	20 ft. 8 in.
Width	6 ft. 11 in. and 6 ft. 0in.	7 ft. 0 in.	6 ft. 9 in.	7 ft. 0 in.	6 ft. 8 in.	8 ft. 2 in.
Height	5 ft. 6 in. and 4 ft. 6 in.	7 ft. 3 in.	7 ft. 9¼ in.	7 ft. 3 in.	9 ft. 5 in.	9 ft. 0 in.
Belly clearance	1 ft. 0 in. or 9 in.	1 ft. 2 in.	1 ft. 4 in.	1 ft. 2 in.	1 ft. 4 in.	1 ft. 7 in.
Armour:						
Front	14-mm. (·551-in.)	28-mm. (1·102-in.)	†25-mm. (·984-in.)	40-mm. (1·574-in.)	40-mm. (1·574-in.)	60-mm. (2·362-in.)
Sides	8-mm. (·315-in.)	24-mm. (·944-in.)	15-mm. (·590-in.)	40-mm. (1·574-in.)	40-mm. (1·574-in.)	60-mm. (2·362-in.)
Top	8-mm. (·315-in.)	12-mm. (·472-in.)	10-mm. (·393-in.)	18-mm. (·708-in.)	15-mm. (·590-in.)	20-mm. (·787-in.)
Armament	One 3·7-cm. (1·45-in.) gun, one M.G.	One 3·7-cm. (1·45-in.) gun, and one 7·92-mm. (·31-in.) M.G. co-axial in turret, one 7·92-mm. (·31-in.) M.G. in hull	One 4·7-cm. (1·85-in.) gun, one 7·92-mm. (·31-in.) M.G. co-axial in turret, one 7·92-mm. (·31-in.) M.G. in hull	One 3·7-cm. (1·85-in.) gun, one M.G. coaxial in turret.	One 4·7-cm. (1·85-in.) gun, one M.G.	One 7·5-cm. (2·95-in.) gun, one 4·7-cm. (1·85-in.) gun, two M.Gs.
Max. speed—m.p.h.	28	22	35	26	29	17
Radius of action—miles	—	72	103	120	125	110
Performance—						
Trench crossing	4 ft. 11 in.	6 ft. 6 in.	6 ft. 5 in.	4 ft. 11 in.	7 ft. 10 in.	9 ft. 0 in.
Step	1 ft. 11 in.	2 ft. 7½ in.	2 ft. 9½ in.	2 ft. 7 in.	2 ft. 11 in.	3 ft. 10 in.
Water forded	2 ft. 7 in.	2 ft. 7½ in.	2 ft. 11½ in.	2 ft. 7 in.	3 ft. 3 in.	4 ft. 10 in.
Max. gradient	45°	28°	28°	40°	40°	40°
Communication	—	W/T, R/T, flag or lamp	W/T	Flag	W/T and R/T	W/T and R/T

* Of these tanks the Czech L.T. 35 S.IIA and L.T.H. tanks and the French Somua tanks are known to be in use with German armoured divisions. The light R.1 and S.1 tanks are included as they might be used, like the Pz.Kw.I tank, as air-borne tanks. The Char B is known to be in production in Occupied France.
† This may have been increased to 50-mm. (1·97-in.).

PRINCIPAL TYPES OF ARMOURED CARS USED BY THE GERMAN ARMY

Type	S.D. Kfz. 222 light 4-wheeled armoured car (2)	A.S.P. 6 medium 6-wheeled armoured car (3)	Heavy 8-wheeled armoured car (4)
Weight—tons	4·7	6·4	9—10
Crew	3	4	4—5
Dimensions—			
Length	15 ft. 7 in.	16 ft. 5½ in.	17 ft. 6 in.
Width	6 ft. 3¾ in.	7 ft. 6 in.—9 ft. 0 in.	8 ft. 0 in.
Height	5 ft. 11½ in.—7 ft. 4¼ in.	8 ft. 0 in. or 9 ft. 0 in.	9 ft. 0 in.
Belly clearance	7¾ in.	—	1 ft. 8 in.
Armour—			
Front	—	—	—
Sides	—	—	—
Top	—	—	—
Thickest plate known	8 mm. (·315-in.) visors: 15-mm. (·59-in.)	14-mm. (·551-in.)	30-mm. (1·181-in.)
Armament	One 2-cm. (·79-in.) super-heavy M.G., one 7·92-mm. (·31-in.) M.G. coaxial in turret	One 2-cm. (·79-in.) super-heavy M.G., one 7·92-mm. (·31-in.) M.G.	One 2-cm. (·79-in.) super-heavy M.G. and one ·79-cm. (·31-in.) M.G.
Max. speed—m.p.h.	31	31	31
Radius of action—miles	124—155	168—216	124—155
Performance estimated—			
Trench crossing	—	—	—
Step	—	—	—
Water forded	—	—	—
Max. gradient	—	—	—
Communication	W/T	W/T and flag	W/T

STANDARD MACHINE CARBINE AND MACHINE GUN

Type	Weight lb.	Rate of fire		Range		Muzzle velocity f.s.	Capacity belt or magazine rounds	Remarks
		Max. r.p.m.	Practical r.p.m.	Max. yards	Effective yards			
(1)	(2)	(3)	(4)	(5)	(6)	(7)	(8)	(9)
i. *Machine carbine* 9-mm. (·35-in.) M.P.38	9·0	520–540	80–90 (Fired in short bursts)	—	Short ranges below 300 yards	1,260	32 (mag.)	Originally designed for use by parachute troops but now in general use as is also a later model —the M.P.40. Six magazines carried in haversack.
ii. *Machine gun* 7·92-mm. (·31-in.) dual purpose M.G.34	26·5	800–900	110–120 (L.M.G.) 300 (Hy. M.G.)	3,281 (direct); 3,828 (indirect) on hy. M.G. mounting	1,650 (on bipod)		50 (belt)	May be used as light or heavy M.G. according to the mounting. Barrel changed after 250 rounds continuous fire. Two or more belts may be joined end to end.

ANTI-TANK RIFLE, ANTI-TANK GUNS AND TANK GUNS

Type	Weight	Practical rate of fire	Muzzle velocity	Weight of projectile	Penetration	Remarks
(1)	(2)	(3)	(4)	(5)	(6)	(7)
i. *Anti-tank rifle* 7·92-mm. (·31-in.) A.Tk. rifle (Pz. B.39)	27·25 lb.	r.p.m. 6–8	f.s. 3,900 (approx.)	lb. ·52 oz.	30·48-mm. (1·2-in.) homogeneous hard plate at 100 yards at normal. Estimated: 22-mm. (·87-in.) armour at 200 yards at normal.	Fires A.P. or A.P. lachrymatory bullet with cemented carbide core. Rifle and ammunition carried by two men.
ii. *Anti-tank guns and tank guns* 2-cm. (·79-in.) super heavy A.A./A.Tk. machine-gun (2-cm. Flak 30).	900 lb.	120	2,625	5·3 oz.	40-mm. (1·57-in.) homogeneous hard plate at 100 yards at normal.	Fires A.P., A.P. incendiary or H.E. shell. M.T. drawn or on S.P. mounting.
2-cm. (·79-in.) A.Tk. gun (Pz. B.41).	501 lb.	8–10	4,555 (approx.)	1·78 oz.	76·2-mm. (3-in.) machinable plate at 100 yards, at normal. 60-mm. (2·36-in.) face-hardened plate at 200 yards at 30°. 50-mm. (1·97-in.) homogeneous hard plate at 300 yards at normal.	Fires A.P. 40* or H.E. Normally towed on trailer. May be split into 5-man load or transport by air.
3·7-cm. (1·45-in.) A.Tk. gun (3·7-cm. Pak).	748 lb.	8–10	2,500	1·68	37-mm. (1·45-in.) N.C. plate at 600 yards at normal. 25-mm. (·98-in.) N.C. plate at 800 yards at 30°.	Fires normal A.P., A.P. 40* or H.E. shell. Towed on own wheels or carried on lorry.
4·7-cm. (1·85-in.) S.P. A.Tk. gun. (4·7-cm. Pak).	7·5 tons	—	3,000	3·75	Estimated: 60-mm. (2·36-in.) armour at 220 yards at normal.	Fires A.P. shell with base fuze and tracer. A.P. 40* or H.E. shell. S.P. mounting (Pz. Kw. I 5·7-ton tank with normal turret removed and a special superstructure substituted).

ANTI-TANK RIFLE, ANTI-TANK GUNS AND TANK GUNS—continued

Type (1)	Weight (2)	Practical rate of fire (3)	Muzzle velocity (4)	Weight of projectile (5)	Penetration (6)	Remarks (7)
		r.p.m.	f.s.	lb.		
5-cm. (1·97-in.) tank gun (5-cm. Kw. K).	—	—	2,600 (estimated)	4·56	Estimated: 63-mm. (2·48-in.) homogeneous tank armour at 200 yards at 30°. 56-mm. (2·2-in.) homogeneous tank armour at 430 yards at 30°.	Fires A.P. shell with base fuze and tracer, A.P. 40* or H.E. shell. Mounted in 18-ton Pz. Kw. III tank.
5-cm. (1·97-in.) A.Tk. gun M./38 (5-cm. Pak 38).	2,016 lb.	—	3,000 (estimated)	4·56	Estimated: 79-mm. (3·11-in.) homogeneous tank armour at 300 yards at 30°. 71-mm. (2·8-in.) homogeneous tank armour at 600 yards at 30°. 63-mm. (2·48-in.) homogeneous tank armour at 850 yards at 30°	Fires A.P. shell with base fuze and tracer, A.P. 40* or H.E. shell. Towed on own wheels.
7·5-cm. (2·95-in.) tank gun (7·5 cm. Kw.K.).	672 lb.	—	1,600 (estimated)	15·3	55-mm. (2·17-in.) homogeneous armour at 400 yards at 30° (estimated).	Fires A.P. shell with base fuze and tracer, H.E. or smoke shell. Mounted in 22-ton Pz. Kw. IV tank.
8·8-cm. (3·46-in.) A.A./A.Tk. gun (8·8 cm.), (Flak 18.)	4·92 tons	15–20	2,690	19·8	Estimated: 100-mm. (3·94-in.) armour at 400 yards at 30°. 70-mm. (2·75-in.) armour at 3,800 yards at normal.	Fires A.P. with percussion fuze, or H.E. with time fuze. M.T. drawn or on S.P. mounting (latter for engagement of ground targets only).

NOTE.—*A.P. 40 ammunition is of a special arrowhead type with a cemented carbide core. It has a good penetration performance at short ranges (up to 400 yards), but has a poor ballistic performance at longer ranges and causes heavy barrel wear.

MORTARS, INFANTRY GUNS AND ASSAULT GUNS

Type (1)	Weight in action (2)	Max. rate of fire (3)	Max. range (4)	Muzzle velocity (5)	Weight of projectile (6)	Range (7)
	lb.	r.p.m.	yards	f.s.	lb.	
i. *Mortars*						
5-cm. (2-in.) mortar (1 Gr. W. 36).	30·8	45	515	262	2·2	One charge only. Max. effective range: 490 yards.
8·1-cm. (3·16-in.) mortar (s.Gr. W. 34).	125	45	2,078	499	7·75	Four charges. Max. effective range: 1,312 yards.
ii. *Infantry guns*						
7·5-cm. (2·95-in.) infantry gun (L.M.W.18.)	780	15–20	3,860 3,780	725 690	12 13·2	Elevation: 72°. Depression: 10°. Traverse: 12°.
15-cm. (5·91-in.) inf. gun (S. Inf. G. 33).	1·5 tons		6,000		80	
iii. *Assault guns*						
7·5-cm. (2·95-in.) assault gun (Sturmgeschütz).			9,000	1,600 (estimated)	14	This is the 7·5-cm. tank gun mounted on Pz. Kw. III chassis. Fires A.P., H.E. and smoke shell.
15-cm. (5·91-in.) assault gun.			6,000		80	This is the heavy infantry gun on a Pz. Kw. I chassis.

DIVISIONAL ARTILLERY WEAPONS

Type (1)	Weight in action (2)	Weight of shell (3)	Muzzle velocity (4)	Maximum range (5)	Degrees elevation (6)	Degrees depression (7)	Degrees traverse (8)	Remarks (9)
10·5-cm. (4·14-in.) gun/how. (L.F.H. 18)	tons 1·9	lb. 32·6	f.s. 1540	yards 11,640	40½	6½	56	Standard field gun/how.
15-cm. (5·91-in.) how. (S.F.H. 18)	4·5	95·7	1970	16,400	50	3	60	Standard medium how.

ANTI-AIRCRAFT GUNS

Type (1)	Weight in action (2)	Muzzle velocity (3)	Max. horizontal range (4)	Max. vertical range (5)	Max. effective ceiling (6)	Time of flight to effective ceiling (7)	Weight of projectile (8)	Rate of fire Theoretical (9)	Rate of fire Practical (10)	Remarks (11)
	lb.	f.s.	yards	feet	feet	secs.	lb.	r.p.m.	r.p.m.	
i. *Light*— 2-cm. (·79-in.) Flak 30 (Rheinmetall).	990	2950	5,230	12,135	7,215	6	0·253	280	120	Dual purpose A.A. and A.Tk. gun.
3·7-cm. (1·45-in.) Flak 36 (Rheinmetall).	tons 1·53	2690	7,085	15,740	13,775	14	1·397	140	60	Dual purpose A.A. and A.Tk. gun M.T. drawn or on S.P. mounting.
ii. *Heavy*— 8·8-cm. (3·46-in.) Flak 18.	4·92	2690	16,200	34,770	34,770	Time of flight not known. In order to provide some indication of safety margin a minimum of 6 secs. to 12,000 ft. may be assumed.	19·8	25	15–20	Krupp, 1934. Standard heavy mobile A.A. gun. Very effective A.Tk. gun.

NEW NOTES
ON THE
GERMAN ARMY

No. 2

CHEMICAL WARFARE AND SMOKE

NOT TO BE PUBLISHED
The information given in this document is not to be communicated, either directly or indirectly, to the Press or any person not holding an official position in His Majesty's Service.

Crown Copyright Reserved

*Prepared under the direction of
The Chief of the Imperial General Staff*

THE WAR OFFICE,
    15th *July*, 1942.

This Document must not fall into Enemy Hands

DISTRIBUTION

All arms	Scale A
G.H.Q., Home Forces	10 copies
Command H.Q. (including A.A.)	5 ,,
London and Northern Ireland districts	5 ,,
Corps H.Q. (including A.A.)	4 ,,
Divisional H.Q. (including A.A.)	3 ,,
Brigade H.Q. (including A.A.)	2 ,,
All group H.Qs.	2 ,,
H.Q., areas, districts, garrisons, sub-areas	1 copy
Intelligence training centre	150 copies
Intelligence training centre (Cambridge Wing)	50 ,,

CONTENTS

	PAGE
Preface	1
Introduction	1

PART I.—ORGANIZATION

SEC. A.—DEFENCE

1. Gas detection	3
2. Decontamination, etc., within the unit	3
3. Special decontamination units	4

B.—OFFENCE

4. Smoke units	5
5. Smoke in other arms	11
6. Gas in other arms	12

PART II.—EQUIPMENT

A.—DEFENCE

7. Personal equipment	16
8. Unit equipment	19
9. Special decontamination equipment	23

B.—OFFENCE

10. Smoke	24
11. Classification of gases	27
12. Offensive gas weapons	28

TABLES

1. Smoke regiment	6
2. Decontamination battery (Contamination battery)	10
3. Scale of issue of decontamination powder	13
4. Ammunition required for a smoke screen of one hour's duration	14
5. Scale of issue of smoke generators and smoke grenades	15
6. Scale of issue of personal anti-gas equipment	16
7. Scale of issue of unit anti-gas equipment	18
8. Identification of gases with detector set	22
9. Types and markings of gas shell	28

Addendum	31

PREFACE

The following chapter of Notes on the German Army—War, 1940, is superseded by the present " New Note ":—

CHAPTER X

In addition, references should be inserted in Chapter XI, para. 3, to the troop decontamination companies, and in Chapter XI, para. 4, to the horse decontamination sections.

INTRODUCTION

Notes on the German Army—War, 1940, gives the organization and equipment of German C.W. and smoke troops as they were believed to be at the time of the Battle of France. Since then considerable developments have taken place in the organization and equipment of these troops, and considerable new information has become available.

General.—The German Government ratified the Geneva Protocol of 1925 prohibiting the use of gas as a weapon of war. It is, however, to be expected that, if the Germans decide that the introduction of gas warfare will be even temporarily to their advantage, they will use gas without hesitation and with their characteristic vigour and thoroughness. Research into chemical warfare has been pursued unremittingly since the last war. The German chemical industry is highly developed, and there is no doubt that the Germans possess ample stocks of war gases, and an adequate supply of trained personnel. Defensive preparations within the army are certainly adequate.

The Germans are thus in a position to begin C.W. at any moment when it may suit them. If they decide to do so, they are unlikely to give any warning, except perhaps in the form of propaganda assertions that gas has been used against them (or the Japanese) by the other side ; such assertions should be taken seriously as an indication.

Organization.—It is now clear that in the event of C.W. breaking out, the offensive role would be borne primarily by the smoke troops, and it is unlikely that there are any specialized C.W. troops outside this arm. The smoke troops are a separate arm of the service, under an Inspectorate of Smoke Troops and Gas Defence (*Inspektion der Nebeltruppe und Gasabwehr*, or *In.9*), which is certainly concerned with the offensive use of gas as well as with gas defence. Smoke troops are organized in general on artillery lines, in regiments, batteries, and troops.

In defence the army possesses, besides the decontamination batteries of the smoke troops, some specialized decontamination companies among the medical troops. Some sections among the veterinary troops specialize in horse decontamination.

Equipment.—Minor developments have occurred in the defensive equipment of the army ; in particular, it is now possible to give some account of German equipment for the detection of gas. In offence, an account can now be given of two new weapons working on the rocket principle, the " smoke mortar d " and the " heavy projector."

PART I.—ORGANIZATION

A.—DEFENCE

1. Gas detection

Anti-gas training is organized on a sound and efficient basis. A number of army anti-gas schools is known, to which officers and N.C.Os. of units are sent for courses; courses are also organized by corps and divisions. Gas exercises, on a fairly large scale, have been reported at various times. Gas equipment is supplied through army anti-gas equipment parks, which belong to the smoke troops.

Each battalion or equivalent unit, and each formation, has a gas defence officer (*Gasabwehroffizier*, abbreviated *Gabo*), who should have attended a gas course; in battalions the duty is generally taken by the " orderly officer " (*Ordonnanzoffizier*). Each unit has also an N.C.O. in charge of anti-gas equipment (*Gasschutzunteroffizier*) whose duties include the training of new personnel as well as the charge of unit anti-gas equipment, the construction of gas chambers, etc. Most units are required to form, from the personnel of their H.Q., a gas-scout section (*Gasspürtrupp*) of a section-leader and three men; battalion and battery H.Q. in mobile troops, artillery, smoke troops, and engineers form two such sections.

Each company or equivalent sub-unit has an anti gas N.C.O., and most sub-units have to form from their own personnel one gas scout section. The anti-gas N.C.O. must not hold any other special office (e.g. the parts of anti-gas N.C.O. and storekeeper must not be doubled), but he can be, and generally is, also the leader of the gas scout section; he should be trained, at least to the extent of having attended an army gas course.

2. Decontamination, etc., within the unit

All troops are equipped on an adequate scale with standard materials for personal and weapon decontamination. The pioneer platoons of infantry regiments (like engineer companies, *see* Sec. 3, para. 5, below and Table 3) are specially equipped with decontamination powder.

Considerable stress is laid by the Germans on the importance of not allowing contaminations to hold up an advance. The gas scout sections are equipped with light anti-gas clothing, and have the duty of reconnoitring and marking off contaminated areas. If the assistance of specialized troops is needed to decontaminate the area through which troops must pass, the area must be reconnoitred beforehand by the troops themselves, and a plan of attack concerted with the specialist troops. Troops are however encouraged to use improvised means of dealing with ground contamination, and units to attack in M.T. over contaminated ground; if vehicles are contaminated, drivers must proceed as fast as possible after decontaminating those parts of their vehicles which they actually need to touch when driving. In extreme cases, an attack may be ordered over contaminated ground without special protection, even at the risk of high gas casualties.

Gas casualties on a small scale are to be dealt with by the unit M.O. If they occur on a large scale, specialized medical companies can be made available. (Apart from these specialized companies, ambulance companies, which are less specialized G.H.Q. troops, are equipped with decontamination materials on a high scale, see Table 3.)

3. Special decontamination units

1. *Decontamination batteries (Entgiftungsabteilungen)* (see Table 2).—These are independent units of the smoke troops in the G.H.Q. pool. The battery is organized as follows :—

Battery H.Q., with signal section and meteorological section.

Three troops.

One decontamination column of nine vehicles, each carrying 1·2 tons of decontamination powder.

The troop organization is :—

Troop H.Q.

Two sections, each with three gas scout sub-sections and six medium decontamination vehicles.

Troop transport (including 400 sets of light A.G. clothing for use of other arms—*see* below).

The ostensible function of the decontamination battery is to co-operate with the infantry in attacking over contaminated ground. The Germans divide this attack into three phases :—

(1) Attack by infantry in light anti-gas clothing (carried by the decontamination battery), to prevent the enemy covering the contaminated area with fire. (It is emphasized that troops engaged in decontamination are extremely vulnerable.)

(2) Clearing of the area by decontamination troops.

(3) Following up of the original attack by further infantry.

For the offensive role of the decontamination batteries *see* Sec. **4**, para. **5**, below.

2. *Road decontamination batteries (Strassenentgiftungsabteilungen)*.—Little is known of these beyond the name. It is presumed that their organization is similar to that of the decontamination batteries.

3. *Troop decontamination companies (Truppenentgiftungskompanien).*—These are motorized companies of medical troops. Details of their organization are not available. They belong to the G.H.Q. pool, and are to be sent wherever high gas casualties have been sustained. They are said to be capable of decontaminating and reclothing 150 men an hour ; they carry 750 sets of replacement clothing and 1,000 sets of " sports clothes " for emergencies.

4. *Horse decontamination sections (Pferdeentgiftungstrupps).* —One of these sections is said to be attached to every veterinary company and every army veterinary hospital. They are motorized, and can be sent where needed by the veterinary officer. Their capacity is said to be 10 to 20 horses an hour.

5. *Engineers.*—All engineer companies carry decontamination powder on a special scale (*see* Table 3). The primary purpose of this allotment is no doubt to enable them to clear contaminated bridges or other engineer installations, but it is probable that the engineers are intended also to help in clearing a passage for infantry through contaminated areas in general. (For the offensive role of the engineers *see* Sec. 6, para. 3, below.)

B.—OFFENCE

4. Smoke units

1. *Smoke regiments (Nebelwerferregimenter)* (*see* Table 1).— The smoke regiment consists of H.Q., signal section and three smoke batteries. The battery contains H.Q., signal section, meteorological section and three troops. Each troop consists of two sections, each of three 10·5-cm. (4·14-in.) smoke mortars (*see* p. 25). The total armament of the normal regiment is thus 54 smoke mortars ; troops of eight and not six mortars are, however, known to occur in some batteries, and the total armament of the regiment might thus rise to anything up to 72 mortars.

The peace strength of a smoke battery was as follows :—

Battery H.Q.	6 officers and 12 O.Rs.
Sig. section	1 officer and 30 O.Rs.
Troop	6 officers and 166 O.Rs.
Total ...	25 officers and 540 O.Rs.

Great importance is attached by the Germans to the primary role of the smoke troops, which are normally allotted to corps as required, for purely smoke purposes. In any large-scale operation smoke will be fired by smoke troops and artillery together, under the control of an artillery commander.

TABLE 1
SMOKE REGIMENT

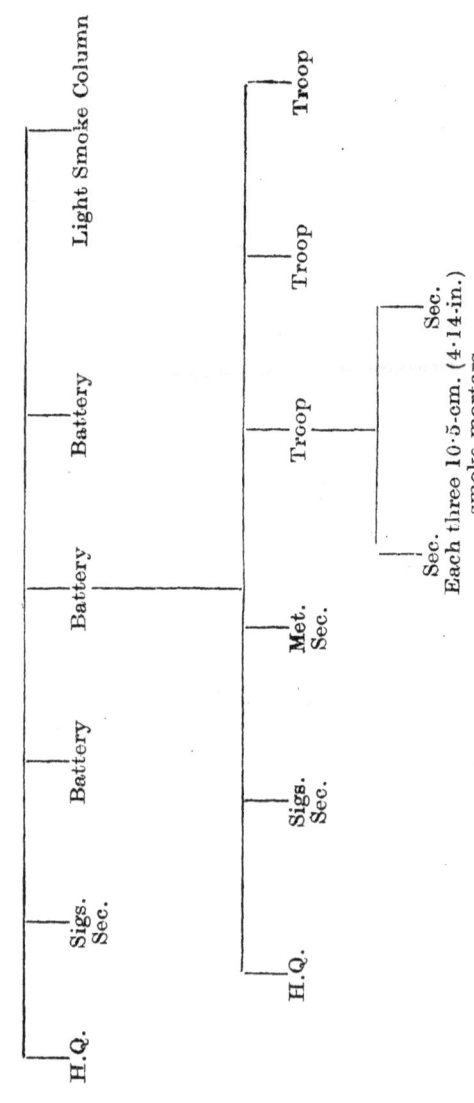

NOTES.—1. The regiment of smoke mortar d has the same organization, except that :—
  i. it is armed with 15-cm. (5·91-in.) **six-barrelled smoke "mortars"** d ;
  ii. there is probably a survey section rather than a meteorological section at battery H.Q.

2. Some troops in the smoke regiment may have sections of four and not three 10·5-cm. (4·14-in.) smoke mortars.

The Germans distinguish between the blinding or preparatory screen (*Blenden oder Vorbereitungsnebel*), and the area screen (*Flächennebel*). The former is laid to blind enemy observation. The latter is laid over an extensive area and fighting is carried out under conditions similar to a natural thick fog. Visibility should be limited to hand grenade range. It will normally be moved forward, as a progressive screen (*Nebelwalze*), according to a fixed time table ; the *average* rate of movement is 220 yards in every 15 minutes. It may be supplemented by the attacking troops themselves with smoke hand grenades or generators, or with mortars and infantry guns. Aircraft may co-operate by attacking targets outside the screen with smoke bombs.

The most favourable wind is a slight headwind, which helps to keep the screen together. Screens can also be laid with a cross wind, but with a following wind the screen tends to straggle away from the attacking troops. It is calculated that in average country a smoke battery of three troops is required on a front of 1,650 yards ; with a side wind a screen of 175 to 240 yards deep can be laid. Ammunition requirements are calculated as follows :—

For every smoke troop, per hour, an average of	1,000 smoke mortar bombs.
Margin, for unfavourable weather...	400 ,, ,,
Total for a smoke battery ...	4,200 ,, ,,

(H.E. ammunition for the smoke mortar is known to exist, but there is no evidence of the scale normally carried.)

The attacking troops must be carefully trained in keeping direction through the screen. The following special means are mentioned :—

i. Wireless navigational beam. This is worked by specially allotted signal troops. The transmitter sends a beam some 20 yards wide ; receivers with the foremost attacking troops determine whether the attack is keeping to the direction of the beam.

ii. Coloured smoke ammunition. This may be specially allotted to the infantry gun companies, in three colours (red, yellow, blue). It is fired, before the attack begins, to land at 50 yards intervals in the direction of the attack.

iii. Guide lines. These are 330 yards long, and are fired by rockets ; they can, if necessary, be fired during the attack along a compass bearing.

iv. Gyro-compass.

v. Guiding strips, in various colours, may be left by the foremost attacking troops as a guide to runners, or troops following up. They may be marked at regular intervals as a guide to the distance reached.

vi. Vertical light signals may be fired by the forward observers of the artillery, who accompany the foremost attacking troops (they are, of course, also provided with wireless apparatus).

It is emphasized that very careful preparation is needed for an attack through smoke. The time-programme of the smoke screen can only be varied if an intermediate objective is fixed, and this can only be done if the intermediate objective is something clearly recognizable, e.g. a road running at right angles to the line of attack.

Attack under cover of smoke across a water obstacle presents special problems; in particular, account must be taken of the difficulties, due e.g. to differing temperature, in the formation of smoke screens on water. Nevertheless, the advantages of smoke are regarded as very great, in covering either the bringing up of boats, etc., or the landing on the opposite bank.

If C.W. breaks out, the primary role will be borne by the smoke regiments. The Germans calculate that a troop of six 10·5-cm. (4·14-in.) smoke mortars is as effective for shooting gas as two troops of 10·5-cm. (4·14-in.) hows.

2. A certain number of independent smoke batteries is also known to exist in the G.H.Q. pool. These can be allotted individually to armies or corps, or a number may be grouped together under an independent regimental H.Q. (*Regimentsstab der Nebeltruppe*)—compare the similar way in which G.H.Q. artillery is often grouped.

3. *Regiment of smoke mortar d (Regiment Nebelwerfer d).*— For this six-barrelled rocket weapon, *see* p. 25 below. At least one regiment equipped with the 15-cm. (5·91-in.) smoke mortar d is already in existence, and it is likely that others will be formed. The organization is similar to that of the normal smoke regiment, perhaps including a survey section at battery H.Q. The regiment possesses in all 54 mortars, but since the smoke mortar d is six-barrelled the regiment can bring to bear greater fire-power in shorter time than the normal smoke regiment; it is claimed that a salvo of 324 rounds can be fired by the regiment every 90 seconds. Independent batteries or troops of smoke mortar d may also be encountered.

The original purpose of this weapon was no doubt to fire smoke, but it appears that its primary role at the present is to attack area targets with H.E. (Like the heavy projector, it is probably somewhat erratic in aim.) It is, however, known that, if C.W. breaks out, the Germans intend to use it to fire gas, and it would clearly be a very effective means of laying down a crash concentration of gas.

4. *Heavy projector (schweres Wurfgerät* 40).—For this rocket weapon *see* p. 25 below. It is known that it forms part of the equipment of the smoke troops, but it is not certainly known to what particular units it is allotted ; probably, like the smoke mortar d, it is the equipment of some specialist unit or units.

Beside the original version of this weapon, whose somewhat cumbrous stand restricted its mobility, the Germans are equipping armoured troop-carrying vehicles to fire the same projectiles, from stands which can be let down from the sides of the vehicle.

These weapons are to be allotted to :—
 i. Such units of lorried infantry as are equipped with armoured troop-carrying vehicles.
 ii. Armoured engineer companies.

There is no evidence, however, to show how far this development has actually taken place.

The primary role of this weapon is to attack area targets with H.E. and incendiary projectiles ; the normal loading consists of five 28-cm. (11-in.) H.E. projectiles and one 32-cm. (12·65-in.) incendiary. It could, however, be used for putting up a concentration of gas.

5. *Contamination batteries* (*Vergiftungsabteilungen*) (*see* Table 2).—These are the decontamination batteries of the smoke troops (*see* Sec. 3, para. 1), converted to contamination batteries by exchanging their decontamination vehicles for bulk contamination vehicles. Until they are required, these bulk contamination vehicles travel in the light decontamination equipment column ; this is *not* the same as the light decontamination column of the decontamination battery (*see* Sec. 3, para. 1), but some form of second-line transport in the smoke troops. The battery is thus able to act at short notice in either role, as a decontamination or as a contamination battery.

The organization of the battery, when converted for contamination, is as follows :—
 Battery H.Q., with signal section and meteorological section.
 3 troops.
 1 light column, of six vehicles each containing 100 portable sprayers.

TABLE 2
DECONTAMINATION BATTERY
(CONTAMINATION BATTERY)

NOTE.—The alterations necessary to convert the decontamination battery into a contamination battery are given in brackets.

```
H.Q.   Sigs.   Met.    Troop           Troop   Troop   Troop
       Sec.    Sec.      |                               |
                         |                               |
                    ┌────┴────┐                    Lt. decontamination coln.
                   H.Q.  Sec.  Sec.                9 vehicles, each 1·2 tons of
                                                   decontamination powder.
              Each 3 gas-scout sub-sections        (6 vehicles, each 100 portable
                 6 medium decontamination vehicles         sprayers.)
             (Each 3 recce. sub-sections
                 6 medium bulk contamination vehicles)
```

Each troop contains :—

Troop H.Q.

2 sections, each of 3 reconnaissance sub-sections and six medium bulk contamination vehicles.

Troop transport.

The German theory of contamination is naturally concerned more with defence and withdrawal than with the attack. In attack, however, it is considered of value for neutralizing centres of enemy resistance which may be by-passed, and safeguarding a flank ; it is also possible, with artillery or aircraft, to hinder an enemy withdrawal or to change its direction, but this possibility is limited by the necessity to avoid hampering the advance of the German troops.

In defence or withdrawal, the Germans draw attention to the obvious value of contamination to hamper an enemy attack or pursuit. They emphasize the importance of contaminating an area of considerable depth and width, and of surprise. The contaminated area must be covered by fire to be fully effective, and in close country it may be necessary to leave troops in or in front of the area ; these can eventually be withdrawn in anti-gas clothing or through gaps. The Germans also contemplate the use of " fake contaminations " (*Scheinvergiftungen*), but these need special equipment, not carried by the normal contamination battery.

Stress is also laid on the necessity of a clear chain of command, and a clear time programme. Normally, a single contamination battery will be under the orders of the formation commander. For very large-scale contaminations, a number of batteries may be grouped together under a special regimental command (*Regimentskommandeur der Nebeltruppe z.b.V.*—compare the independent smoke batteries above, p. 8).

5. Smoke in other arms

1. *Artillery.*—It is believed that the Germans consider the dispersion of smoke by artillery weapons uneconomical, as the latter are thereby prevented from carrying out their primary role. Smoke shell is, however, still carried by artillery units ; the scale varies, but that laid down is normally about 25 per cent. of the total ammunition carried.

For a progressive smoke screen, artillery are required as follows :—

On a front of 160 yds.   One troop of 10·5-cm. (4·14-in.) hows.

,,   ,,   ,,   220 ,,   One troop of 15-cm. (5·91-in.) hows.

,,   ,,   ,,   1,650 ,,   Six troops of 10·5-cm. (4·14-in.) hows. *and* three troops of 15-cm. (5·91-in.) hows.

For ammunition requirements, *see* Table 4.

2. *Tanks and other armoured vehicles.*—Every armoured vehicle carries five smoke generators (*see* Sec. 10, para. 2, ii, below) as part of its normal equipment.

3. *Engineers.*—All engineer units and sub-units, with the exception of bridging columns, carry smoke generators; armoured units and sub-units also carry smoke hand grenades. For the scale, *see* Table 5.

4. *Infantry, etc.*—All infantry regiments, and certain other units and sub-units, carry smoke generators; some also carry smoke hand grenades. For the scale, *see* Table 5.

It should be noted that assault detachments (Notes on the German Army—War, 1940, p. 29) normally include a smoke party of two to three men armed with smoke generators and smoke hand grenades; these may be infantry pioneers or divisional engineers.

Smoke can also be fired by the 8·1-cm. (3·16-in.) mortar used by the infantry, and by the light or heavy infantry gun; it does not, however, appear that infantry units regularly carry smoke ammunition for these weapons. There is no evidence of smoke ammunition for the 5-cm. (2-in.) mortar.

5. *Aircraft.*—Many reports have referred to G.A.F. training in the production of smoke clouds, and containers varying in content from 20 gallons to over 60 gallons have been described. Instructions on the use of the *S* 300 (p. 27) are that the smoke should be released at a height of 100 feet and that a smoke cloud about 10 miles long can be laid. It is thus apparent that the intention is to create a cloud, rather than a curtain.

Reference has also been made to smoke bombs (*see* p. 7).

6. Gas in other arms

1. *Artillery.*—The Germans are known to regard the smoke mortar as more effective than artillery weapons for firing gas (*see* above, p. 8), but it is certainly intended that artillery shall play a large part if C.W. breaks out. The Germans are known to have built up large stocks of gas shell, and to have devoted considerable attention to the technique of gas bombardment.

Details of the proposed allotment of gas shell to the artillery are not available, but it is known that the principal part is to be played by the 10·5-cm. (4·14-in.) gun hows. and the 15-cm. (5·91-in.) hows. of the divisional artillery. These will fire gas shell of all types. It is to be noted that most German gas shells now have a relatively high H.E. content and produce a considerable splinter effect (up to 90 per cent. of the pure H.E. shell); it is not possible to distinguish gas from H.E. shell by the sound of the explosion.

The Germans distinguish the following types of gas bombardment :—

A.—*Bombardments for cloud effect*

i. Surprise—to put the enemy out of action before A.G. measures can be adopted.
ii. Neutralizing—bombardment for several hours, or even days, to neutralize enemy units, weaken their gas discipline and so inflict casualties.
iii. Harassing—intermittent bombardment, to compel the wearing of the respirator over a long period and weaken gas discipline.
iv. Interpolation of gas ammunition into H.E. or smoke bombardment.

B.—*Contamination bombardments*

2. *Infantry.*—Lachrymatory gas ammunition will also be issued for the 8·1-cm. (3·16-in.) infantry mortar and the 7·5-cm. (2·95-in.) light infantry gun ; and blister gas shell for the 15-cm. (5·91-in.) heavy infantry gun.

3. *Infantry pioneer platoons, and engineers.*—Blister gas will be issued to infantry pioneers and to engineer units to enable them to contaminate the neighbourhood of road-blocks, etc., in order to make them more effective obstacles.

4. *Aircraft.*—The Germans regard aerial spray as a most effective weapon and should the use of C.W. methods commence, the German Air Force will bear a heavy weight of the offensive. Smoke curtain installations exist, which can, by very slight modification, be used to release blister gas. Although few details are available there can be no doubt that the enemy is also adequately supplied with gas bombs of all types.

TABLE 3

SCALE OF ISSUE OF DECONTAMINATION POWDER

H.Qs. down to bn., bty., etc.	... each	5	22-lb. canisters
H.Qs. of engineer battalions	... each	8	,, ,,
Railway engineer coys. ...	... each	8	,, ,,
Construction coys., ...	... each	8	,, ,,
All other eng. coys. ...	*per platoon*	8	,, ,,
Infantry pioneer platoons (horsed)	each	6	,, ,,
Mechanized pioneer platoons ...	each	5	,, ,,
Ambulance coys.	each	30	,, ,,

Anti-gas equipment parks also store 55-lb. and 112-lb. barrels.

TABLE 4
AMMUNITION REQUIRED FOR A SMOKE SCREEN OF ONE HOUR'S DURATION

	Width of front (yds.)	Troops of artillery	Smoke shell needed to form area screen	Smoke shell needed to maintain area screen	
				In favourable weather	In unfavourable weather
Preparatory Screen	160	Tp. of 10·5-cm. how.	8–16	240	360
	220	Tp. of 15-cm. how.	4–8	120	240
	990 / 660	6 tps. of 10·5-cm. how. / 3 tps. of 15-cm. how.	— / —	1440 / 360	2160 / 720
Progressive Screen	160	Tp. of 10·5-cm. how.	20	480	720
	220	Tp. of 15-cm. how.	20	240	480
	990 / 660	6 tps. of 10·5-cm. how. / 3 tps. of 15-cm. how.	— / —	2880 / 720	4320 / 1440

TABLE 5

SCALE OF ISSUE OF SMOKE GENERATORS AND SMOKE HAND GRENADES

1. Engineers

	Smoke generators	Smoke hand grenades
Armd. eng. bn.	564	315
Other eng. bns.	792	—
Armd. eng. coy.	144	40
Other eng. coys.	156	—
Lt. eng. coln. in armd. div.	108	225
Lt. eng. coln. in other divs.	324	—

2. Other arms

	Smoke generators	Smoke hand grenades
Inf. regt.	144	—
Inf. pnr. pl.*	—	15
Mech. pnr. pl.	48	15
M.G. bn.	288	135
Coy. of M.G. bn.	—	15
Lorried inf. regt.	144	—
Lorried inf. or M.C. bn.	72	—
All A.Tk. coys.	12	—
Armd. car sqns.	192	—
Armd. car tp.	56	—

* Not including pioneer platoons of mountain regiments.

TABLE 6

SCALE OF ISSUE OF PERSONAL ANTI-GAS EQUIPMENT
(Reference Sec. **7**)

Para.	Article	Scale of Issue	Where carried
1.	Respirator, complete.	1 per person.	On the person.
2.	Anti-gas ointment (Losantin).	4 boxes, each of 10 tablets, per person.	On the person, in the breast pocket of the field tunic.
3.	Anti-gas sheet in pouch.	1 per person.	On the person, on the chest or around the respirator carrier.
4.	Respirator spectacles and anti-dim.	1 each person who requires to wear spectacles.	In the respirator carrier.
5.	Pocket flask of weapon decontaminant.	1 flask per person.	In the breast pocket of the field tunic with screw cap uppermost.

PART II.—EQUIPMENT

A.—DEFENCE

7. Personal equipment

(For the scale of personal equipment carried, *see* Table 6.)

1. *Respirators.*—The German service respirator comprises facepiece, directly attached drum container, and carrier. All service types are derived from the German S mask, itself based on the pattern used in the war of 1914–1918 :—

i. *Facepieces.*—The facepieces in present use are of two types—the *G.M.*30 (and earlier models) and the *G.M.*38. The *G.M.*30 is made of a duplex material (a canvas outer layer, a layer of rubber, a layer of closely woven cotton fabric, and an inner layer of rubber) with a fitting band of suede leather and adjustable head harness of webbing and steel springs. A carrying band is provided for an alert position. The removable eyepieces are of cellulose acetate, and replaceable gelatine coated anti-dimming discs are fitted to the inside of these by rings. A rubber disc inlet valve and a spring-loaded mica disc outlet valve, together with a protective grid, are housed in the container attachment piece which is screwed to receive the neck of the container. Facepieces are provided in three sizes. The *G.M.*38 is an all-rubber moulded facepiece similar in general design and shape to the earlier model. The fitting band, also of rubber, is an integral part of the moulding, while the head harness is of much simpler design, and a hanging tab is provided. The eyepieces are not removable.

ii. *Containers*.—The containers are all similar in general design, being drum types made of grey-green painted tinned plate with either perforated or single hole baseplates. Earlier models (S and Getr) were filled with three different layers, a top layer of brick granules impregnated with potassium carbonate and hexamine, a centre layer of charcoal, and at the bottom a cotton asbestos filter pad. In all later models the upper layer of granules is replaced by a further layer of charcoal.

A *non-magnetic container* has been issued to units equipped with compasses. This differs from the ordinary container only in the replacement of the tinned plate of the body by non-magnetic metal. The main marking of this is a brown band, 1 cm. wide, around the centre. Troops in the Middle East and similar theatres of war are equipped with *special tropical containers*, marked *TROPEN*. The base plate of the standard container has been redesigned, the normal perforated plate being replaced by a slightly domed base with a central circular orifice as inlet. This may be closed by a rubber bung.

A new container and a non-magnetic equivalent have recently been released for issue. These are identical with the tropical models in appearance, that is, with a single orifice in the base.

iii. *Carriers*.—The *standard carrier* is a metal cylinder, with lid fitted with a quick release fastening, carried by a web sling from the shoulder. A cleaning rag is carried at the bottom, and a compartment on the underside of the lid holds the spare anti-dimming discs.

A *carrier of grey canvas* with an aluminium " zip " fastener, to open at the side, is also in use, but is probably intended only for parachute or air-landing troops. The spare anti-dimming discs are carried in a pocket on the side of the carrier.

Special spectacle frames with flat metal and tape side members are provided to those who require to wear spectacles under their facepieces.

2. *Anti-gas ointment (Losantin)*.—All German troops are equipped with four small brown bakelite boxes (3 in. × 1 in. × ½ in.), each containing ten tablets of Losantin, a high quality stabilized bleaching powder. The method of use is to mix one of the tablets with water or saliva and to apply the paste so formed to the affected skin.

TABLE 7

SCALE OF ISSUE OF UNIT ANTI-GAS EQUIPMENT

(Reference Sec. 8)

Para.	Article	Scale of Issue	Where carried
1, i	Protective clothing, light.	Gas scout sections, each 4 sets. Unit H.Q., spares 8 sets	A echelon. B echelon.
1, ii	Protective clothing, heavy.	Special units only.	
2, i	Decontamination canisters.	*See* Table 3.	Combatant troops, A echelon, other units, unit transport.
2, ii	Weapon decontamination outfit.	Coys., etc., each ... 4 Unit H.Q. 1	A echelon. A echelon.
3, i	Detector powder (55 lb. drums).	Unit H.Q. 1	A echelon.
3, ii	Detector canisters.	Gas scout sections, each 4 Unit H.Q., spares ... 4	A echelon. B echelon.
3, iii	Detector pump.	No evidence of allotment.	
3, iv	Spray detector cards.	No evidence of allotment.	
3, v	Flags, warning, gas.	Gas scout sections, each 4 sets Unit H.Q., spares 4 sets	A echelon. B echelon.
3, vi	Detector sets.	Gas scout sections, each 1	
4.	Whistling cartridges.	10 per signal pistol. (Normal allotment of signal pistols :— Coy. H.Q. ... ... 1 Rifle platoon ... ... 1 M.G. or mortar section ... ... 1 Unit H.Q. ... ... 4)	With signal ammunition.
5.	Gas runners.	No evidence of allotment.	
6.	Anti-gas helmet.	Unit H.Q. ... ... 6 Regt. H.Q. coys. ... 1	With medical equipment.
7.	Oxygen breathing set.	No evidence.	As far as possible with A echelon.
	Sets of spare respirators.	Coys., etc., each ... 2 Unit H.Q. 1	

3. *Anti-gas sheet.*—The anti-gas sheet is intended to be used either as a protection against spray from aircraft or as a groundsheet when lying on contaminated ground. It consists of a plain rectangular sheet of a treated fabric, approximately 6 ft. 6 in. × 4 ft. in size, which folds up and is carried in a small pouch, measuring 8 in. × 6 in. × 1 in., either slung across the chest or fastened around the respirator carrier. The earlier anti-gas sheets were made of waxed or creped paper, but the present issue is of " rubberized " fabric, those for ordinary theatres being black, and the tropical model (marked Tp) a light khaki. To gain protection from spray the man crouches or kneels and throws the sheet over his head so that it covers him.

4. *Pocket flask of weapon decontaminant.*—Each man is supplied with a pocket flask of weapon decontaminant for decontamination of his personal weapons and equipment. (For details *see* Sec. 8, para. 2, ii, Decontamination equipment.)

5. *Eyeshields.*—There is no evidence of eyeshields having been issued.

8. Unit equipment

(The scale of issue of unit anti-gas equipment is given in Table 7.)

1. *Protective clothing*

i. *Light anti-gas clothing.*—A suit of German light anti-gas clothing consists of a combination jacket with short trunks, leggings which cover most of the upper of the boot and extend nearly to the crutch, a hood, and light anti-gas gloves. The complete set is packed in a satchel similar to that for the anti-gas sheet though larger (10 in. by 16 in.). The leggings are donned first, followed by the jacket, the trunks being used as step-ins, over the leggings. The arms are inserted and the garment fastened by a stud at the back of the neck (this leaves the back uncovered). The hood is conical with an opening for the respirator, and is put on over the respirator and steel helmet. A rubber ring attached above the mask opening is drawn down over the steel helmet to keep the hood in position. The hood extends well down over the chest, shoulders, and back. The gauntlets of the gloves extend to the elbows and rubber bands are slipped over the wrists.

ii. *Heavy anti-gas clothing.*—The Germans also have heavy anti-gas clothing, which consists of a two-piece suit of jacket with attached hood and trousers made of a heavy grey-coloured rubber fabric. Heavy gloves and overboots or Wellingtons probably complete the issue.

2. *Decontamination equipment*

i. *Ground.*—Bleaching powder is the usual substance for ordinary decontamination. Losantin, in powder form, is normally used, though the Germans teach that commercial bleaching powder will be used if Losantin is not available. Losantin, or bleaching powder, is either strewn by hand or by decontamination canisters, or on a larger scale by decontamination vehicles. It may also be used as a bleach paste.

The *decontamination canister* is supplied in two models, one of papier mâché, the other of metal. The canister is in the form of a square box with a fixed bottom. At the top there is a large circular hole fitted with a detachable sieve and a lid.

Capacity : 22 lb. of decontaminant.

To operate, the lid is removed, the canister turned upside down, and either shaken or swung over the ground to be decontaminated.

Decontamination vehicles are special equipments (*see* Sec. **9**) operated by the decontamination batteries (p. 4).

ii. *Weapons.*—A special *liquid weapon decontaminant* is issued for use on delicate weapons and apparatus. It is supplied in the *weapon decontamination outfit*. Further each man is issued with a *pocket flask* of the liquid for the decontamination of his personal weapons and equipment.

The weapon decontamination outfit comprises a cylindrical tin containing one jar of weapon decontaminant, one of cleaning oil, and cloths and brushes for applying the decontaminant and oil.

The pocket flask is a small flat dropping bottle, made of synthetic material closed by a fluted screw cap. Pressure on the sides expels drops of the liquid.

iii. *Clothing.*—The normal method used by the Germans for decontamination of clothing is steam treatment, although any of the general methods of decontamination (boiling, etc.) may be employed as an emergency measure. *Mobile decontamination plant* for such decontamination forms part of the equipment of special units (*see* Sec. **3**, para. 3).

3. *Detector equipment.*—The equipment available to units of the German army for carrying out the duties of gas detection comprise the following :—

Detector powder, used either from a detector canister or a detector pump.
Spray detector cards.
Set of flags, warning, gas.
Gas detector set.

i. *Detector powder* is a pink or yellowish dry powder consisting of fine silica to which have been added dye and reactive materials. If the detector powder is strewn over the contaminated area it absorbs a portion of the liquid gas with which it comes into contact, and in doing so becomes coloured red brown if the contaminant is mustard gas, or blue with lewisite, either immediately or within a few minutes.

ii. *Detector canister.*—This is a cylindrical papier mâché container. A handgrip and a carrying strap are attached to the fixed top lid. The bottom is provided with a filling hole and dredger holes of two different sizes, carried on a rotatable disc. Beneath this there is firmly fixed a disc with a section removed, so that by turning the perforated disc by means of the handle the section can be brought into register with the filling hole or dredger holes, or the canister can be closed.

Weight : empty, 1·3 lb. ; full, 4.8 lb.
Diameter : 5 in. Height : 10 in.
Length of detector trace with large dredging holes : 165 yds.
Length of detector trace with small dredging holes : 220 yds.

In order to strew the powder the end disc is turned in such a way that either the large or small holes are open, the canister gripped by the handgrip and shaken up and down if an individual point is being tested, or swung vigorously to and fro to lay a trace.

iii. *The detector pump* serves to detect areas of contamination which cannot be reached by means of the detector canister (e.g. on vehicles). It blows out detector powder in a thin stream. The pump looks like a British service respirator container, though larger, with a carrying handle on one round edge and a carrying strap on the other. At the top there is a flat pump handle and on the bottom a filling hole with screw cap, and the jet by which the powder is expelled.

Weight : empty, 2·6 lb. ; full, 5·7 lb.

iv. *Spray detector cards* are issued in packets of twenty, together with an instruction card, which shows the colour changes to be expected with various gases and other chemicals which may be encountered (smoke acid, mineral oil, etc.). The cards are of thick cardboard (8 in. by 10 in.) treated on both sides with a pink coloured mustard sensitive paint. The use envisaged by the Germans is the same as that of our detectors, gas, spray.

v. *Set of flags, warning, gas.*—This is intended to mark areas of ground found to be contaminated, and comprises 20 flags, a roll of marking tape, and a carrying satchel. The warning flag consists of a long iron rod, the top of which is bent at right angles to form a pointer from which is suspended a triangular yellow cloth flag bearing the skull and crossbones device. The upright part of the rod is provided with two eyes so that one warning flag can be mounted above a second. The marking tape is a ribbon ¾ in. wide, dyed yellow, approximately 50 yards of which are provided on a papier mâché bobbin.

If a gas scout has confirmed that the ground is contaminated he retires and places a warning flag on uncontaminated ground about 6 yards from the edge of the contamination. The recommended interval is 20–60 yards.

vi. *The gas detector set* is a more complicated apparatus issued to, and used by, the leader of the gas scout section. Whereas the equipment already described is intended to be used when ground contamination is suspected, the gas detector set identifies individual gases present either as airborne vapours and gases, or as ground contamination. The gas scout sucks the air to be tested, by means of a suction pump, through testing tubes which contain detector materials.

These tubes are made of synthetic transparent material, and contain at the upper end one or two ampoules of liquid reagent, one or two white or pale yellow test layers and finally a brownish absorbent layer. The tubes are closed at each end by discs of plastic, which are thin in the middle so that they can be easily punctured for insertion into the pump head when used.

A special testing tube is provided for each group of war gases. It is thus necessary for several tests to be made one after another. The tubes are marked with coloured bands, and Table 8 indicates the gases identifiable.

TABLE 8

Tube No.	Colour of marking bands	Gas detected	Colour change
1	One yellow	Mustard	To orange-yellow
2	Two yellow	Arsine	Lower layer to yellow-brown
3	One green	Phosgene and diphosgene	To green-blue
4	Two green	Chloropicrin	To pink or red
5	One black	Cyanides	To blue

4. *Gas alarm.* —The Germans intend to use whistling cartridges, fired from the signal pistol, as a general gas alarm.

Local alarms taught by the German gas school are :—
Non-persistent gas. The mask is put on and the carrier held aloft.
Persistent gas. The rifle and the carrier are held aloft.

5. *Gas runner.*—As an aid to the traversing of contaminated areas, units are equipped with the gas runner. This is simply a roll of strong impregnated paper, 55 yards long and 4 feet wide, rolled on to a cardboard cylinder. It is resistant to mustard gas and water, and, with careful use, 200 men can cross by it before its life is ended. It can be used on one occasion only and must then be destroyed.

6. *Anti-gas helmet.*—Among the unit medical equipment, the anti-gas helmet is intended to be worn by personnel with head wounds, who are unable, because of these wounds, to wear a normal type of facepiece. It consists of a thin rubber loosely fitting hood, completely covering the head and neck, with a large oval window in the front. It is fitted with tying bands, which ensure a gastight fit, a simple outlet valve, and an inlet valve, to which a service container is fitted. It is normally carried in a flat square metal tin.

7. *Oxygen breathing set.*—A very good self-contained one-hour oxygen breathing set has been standardized by the Germans, and called the "*Heeresatmer.*" This consists of the usual oxygen cylinder, breathing bag, alkali cartridge, and valves, and is used with an ordinary facepiece.
Weight 26 lb.
It is completely contained in a metal case (15 in. by 14 in. by 6 in.) carried on the back.

9. Special equipment for decontamination

1. Special equipment exists in the German army for the large scale decontamination of ground, clothing, and personnel.

2. *Ground decontamination.*—Small and medium semi-tracked vehicles, equipped at the rear with hoppers for distributing bleaching powder, are to be used. The loading spaces of the vehicles are packed with drums of decontamination material, to be fed into the hopper, and sixteen canisters (p. 20) for the decontamination of isolated areas by hand are also carried.

The medium vehicle, which forms the main equipment of the decontamination batteries (p. 4), carries $\frac{3}{4}$ ton of bleaching powder and can decontaminate a path 5 feet wide and nearly a mile long.

3. *Decontamination of clothing.*—The clothing decontamination vehicle is a large, closed six-wheeled lorry. It probably

carries a boiler for generating steam quickly, a steam chamber, and a drying chamber. Contaminated uniforms are cleansed in the steam chamber and dried in the drying chamber with hot air, also produced by the lorry.

4. *Decontamination of personnel.*—Although the German soldier is responsible for his personal decontamination, special medical companies (*see* p. 5) exist, to be used in localities where gas casualties are numerous and severe. The equipment of these companies include heavy six-wheeled road lorries, resembling horse boxes in appearance and probably incorporating some form of bath equipment.

B.—OFFENCE
10. Smoke

1. The enemy attaches great importance to the proper use of smoke in warfare, and is adequately provided with weapons for the creation of screens, both large and small.

The normal marking for smoke ammunition is a broken white line, and lettering, including Nb, also in white (e.g. Nb. Hgr. 39 in white, above a wide white line broken into four segments, is the marking of the smoke hand grenade 39).

2. *General equipment.*—The following types of smoke equipment are likely to be used by all arms. For scales of issue *see* Table 5 (scale of issue of spray-type smoke generators is not known).

i. *Hand grenades.*—The *smoke hand grenade* 39 closely resembles the model 24 H.E. " *Stielhandgranate* " (Notes on the German Army—War, p. 58), the metal head of which has been replaced by one filled with Berger type smoke mixture. Duration of emission 1 to 2 minutes.

The *smoke hand grenade* 41 consists of a small smoke generator in a cylindrical metal casing weighing about $1\frac{1}{4}$ lb. No handle is fitted.

ii. *Smoke generators* (thermal type).—Two smoke generators of this type (*Nebelkerze*) are in general service use. These are the *model* 39 and the *model S*. Both consist of a green painted cylinder $5\frac{3}{4}$ in. high and $3\frac{1}{2}$ in. in diameter, fitted with a small screwhole at one end for the insertion of the igniter. Model 39 also has a carrying handle, which folds flat on to the lid. The generator is filled with Berger mixture, and has a time of emission of 4 to 7 minutes.

Markings (in white) are :—
  Model 39.—Nb. K-39 over a broken white band.
  Model S.—Nb.K.S. 39 over two broken white bands.

iii. *Smoke generators* (*spray type*).—In 1933 two models, a large and a small, of spray type smoke generator were introduced, and their use in training was strongly advocated. Few details of these models are available, and it is considered that they are now obsolescent.

In 1941 a new type, the *smoke generator* 41 (*Nebelzerstäuber* 41) was introduced for trial. It was designed to screen single buildings, bridges, battery positions, and the like, for long periods (up to two hours), and for large back area screens.

The generator is in the form of a strong walled iron drum fitted externally with a stopcock and a steel projection tube. The cylinder of compressed air necessary to expel the smoke acid (20 gallons of a mixture of chlorsulphonic acid and sulphur trioxide) is probably contained within the drum. The empty weight is 280 lb.

3. *Equipment of smoke troops*

i. *Smoke mortars* (*Nebelwerfer*).—The normal armament of the smoke battery (*see* p. 5) is the 10·5-cm. (4·14-in.) smoke mortar, of which two models, the " 35 " and the " 40," are known. The earlier of these closely resembles a " Stokes " mortar and fires a streamlined bomb a distance of about 3,000 yards. The rate of fire and capacity of the projectile are not known, but it is probable that the former does not exceed 20 rounds a minute. Few details are known of the model " 40." The maximum range is some 6,500 yards.

ii. *Rocket projectiles.*—At least two weapons, operating on the rocket principle, have been recently introduced for use by the smoke troops. Of these the smoke mortar d is undoubtedly for use with gas and smoke projectiles, although H.E. rounds are available ; the heavy projector is only known to fire H.E. and incendiary rounds, and there is as yet no indication that smoke and gas ammunition is to be available.

Smoke mortar d* (*Nebelwerfer d*) (*see* p. 8).—This *weapon* resembles a small gun, and has six barrels arranged in a circle in a similar manner to the chambers of a revolver. The mounting consists of a pair of rubber tyred wheels and a split trail. The barrels are not rifled but have straight guide rails within them. The projectiles are 15-cm. (5·91-in.) calibre rockets, shaped like artillery shells. The six rounds from one weapon are fired electrically at intervals of one second. The rate of fire, including the time required to reload, is six rounds (one from each barrel) every 90 seconds.

Maximum range 6,670 yards.

H.E., smoke, and gas charged ammunition is available.

Heavy projector (*schweres Wurfgerät* 40) (*see* pp. 9, 32).—Two forms of this weapon are known. In the original form issued

---

* It is, of course, not a mortar, but for convenience the German name is here retained.

to smoke troops the projectiles were fired from a heavy wooden frame. It is possible that this form of the projector is still in use by smoke troops, but a new form has now been introduced, consisting of six projector frames mounted on a medium armoured semi-tracked vehicle, three on each side. The frames can be elevated (to a maximum of 42 degrees) but not traversed, so that the weapon is aimed by pointing the vehicle at the target. It is fired electrically, projectiles leaving stands at intervals of two seconds; hence a series of six rounds, one from each stand, takes 10 seconds. Six rounds are carried on the vehicle, of which five are usually H.E. and the sixth incendiary.

Ammunition	Calibre	Weight	Filling
H.E.	28-cm. (11-in.)	181 lb.	110 lb. T.N.T.
Incendiary.	32-cm. (12·6-in.)	174 lb.	11 galls. of oil.

Maximum range 2,000 yards, minimum 1,000 yards.

As yet there is no evidence that smoke ammunition is available.

iii. A *special smoke vehicle*, built on a 3-ton semi-tracked chassis, is known to exist, but as far as can be ascertained its sole function is to carry a large number of smoke generators in racks, from which they may be rapidly removed for use.

4. *Smoke equipment in other arms*

i. *Artillery.*—Both the 10·5-cm. (4·14-in.) and the 15-cm. (5·91-in.) *field howitzers* fire smoke shell, as does the 7·5-cm. (2·95-in.) assault gun (*Sturmgeschütz*) (New Notes on the German Army—No. 1, p. 30). The following ammunition is known :—

Gun	Shell	Weight of shell	Charging	Colour of body	Marking
10·5-cm. fd. how. (1.F.H. 18)	Fd. how. smoke	30 lb.	Pumice soaked in oleum ?	Field grey	" Nb " (2·4 in. high) stencilled in white, on both sides of cylindrical portion.
Ditto.	Fd. how. shell 38 smoke	32 lb.	Ditto.	Ditto.	" 38 Nb ".
15-cm. fd. how. (s.F.H. 18)	Fd. how. smoke		13 lb. pumice soaked in oleum.		
7·5-cm. assault gun		14 lb.	Pumice soaked in oleum	Dark green	" Nb " (2·4 in. high) stencilled in white above driving band.

ii. *Infantry.*—Smoke ammunition is fired by the following infantry weapons, but no details are available :—

3·1-cm. (3·16-in.) *mortar* (*s.Gr.W.*34) (New Notes on the German Army—No. 1, p. 30).

7·5-cm. (2·95-in.) *light infantry gun* (New Notes on the German Army—No. 1, p. 30).

15-cm. (5·91-in.) *heavy infantry gun* (New Notes on the German Army—No. 1, p. 30).

iii. *Tank units.*—All tanks are fitted, at the rear, with a smoke rack from which five generators can be operated. This rack is intended for the individual protection of the tank, and it is doubtful if it could be used for the support of other arms (e.g. infantry).

In addition, the 7·5-*cm. gun*, fitted in the main turret of the Pz.Kw.IV medium tank, fires the same smoke shell as the 7·5-cm. assault gun.

iv. *Engineer units.*—There is no indication that engineers employ special smoke equipment, although they are issued with the normal weapons on a higher scale than other arms (*see* Table 5). Smoke generators (spray type) would obviously be of considerable use in many engineer activities (e.g. bridge building).

v. *Aircraft.*—Smoke-producing installations of several types are known. Two types of gravity-operated spray apparatus, suitable for either smoke or gas, were produced by a Czech firm and are now available to the enemy; their capacities are respectively 20 and 42 gallons. Reports have also described an apparatus called the *V* 200, suitable for use with both smoke and gas, of 44 galls. capacity, and weighing about 500 lb.

A larger apparatus, the *S* 300, is intended primarily for the laying of smoke screens. It is a pressure operated weapon, consisting of a cylindrical container, with inset compressed air bottle, and complete with the necessary control valves, and an emission pipe. The emission is operated electrically from a switchbox near the observer's seat and can be interrupted at will. In the Dornier 217 it is carried in the bomb stowage compartment.

It is considered that several types of German aircraft could be fitted with smoke equipment.

11. Classification of gases

1. The German classification of gases in use during the last war has persisted, at least in teaching, to the present day. This classification may be summarized as follows :—

British classification	German classification
Blister gases	Yellow cross (*Gelbkreuz*)
Choking gases	Green cross (*Grünkreuz*)
Nose gases (toxic smokes)	Blue cross (*Blaukreuz*)
Tear gases	White cross (*Weisskreuz*)

2. The substances considered by the Germans in their

teaching are essentially the same as those which the British place in the same class, although in the last war German preferences did not always agree with our own ; thus among the nose gases they preferred DA and DC to DM, and used brominated compounds (bromacetone, etc.) as tear gases.

3. There is strong evidence that, when applied as code markings to weapons, some alteration has been made to the above classification. Crosses may have been superseded by *rings*, and some gases, which combine the properties of two groups, marked with two rings of different colours. Thus a charging with *green* and *yellow* rings indicates a choking gas with vesicant properties, and a *double yellow ring* a vesicant of enhanced persistence.

Among the chargings believed to exist the following are of interest :—

The *white ring*, or tear gas, charging, effective in low concentrations, is somewhat persistent and smells of almonds.

One of the *green ring* chargings has little smell, and two others are said to have a faint smell resembling mustard gas. All green ring chargings have a limited vesicant effect.

12. Offensive gas weapons

1. *General.*—Research in chemical warfare methods has been almost continuous since the last war. Marked attention has been given to aerial and ground methods of contamination, suggesting that, where these weapons can be used, they are considered more efficient and economical than artillery shell for the dispersion of gas. Recently, at least one new gas weapon, the smoke mortar d (*Nebelwerfer d, see* p. 25, above) has been introduced. The development of further gas weapons, or the considerable improvement of weapons already well known, cannot be ignored.

TABLE 9
TYPES AND MARKINGS OF GAS SHELL

Marking	Type of shell	Calibre
Yellow ring (obsolescent)	Gas	10·5 cm. and 15 cm. (fd. how.)
Double yellow ring ...	Gas	,,
Blue ring 1	Gas/HE	10·5 cm. and 15 cm. (fd. how.)
Blue ring 2	Gas/HE	10·5 cm. (fd. how.)
Green ring (obsolescent)	Gas/HE	15 cm. (inf. gun), 10·5 cm. and 15 cm. (fd. how.)
Green ring 1 38 ...	Gas/HE	10·5 cm. (fd. how.)
Green ring yellow 38 ...	Gas/HE	15 cm. (inf. gun), 10·5 cm. and 15 cm. (fd. how.)
White ring	Gas/HE	7·5 cm. (inf. gun), 10·5 cm. and 15 cm. (fd. how.)

2. *Weapons of smoke troops*

i. The 10·5-cm. (4·14-in.) *smoke mortar*, which is the normal armament of the smoke battery, is intended to fire gas as well as smoke.

The following *ammunition* is believed to exist :—
Yellow ring.
Double yellow ring.

It must be assumed that smoke mortars will not be limited in use to the dispersion of blister gas, and it is therefore probable that ammunition with any of the markings shown in Table 9 will be available.

ii. Gas ammunition for the smoke mortar d (*see* p. 25, above) is known to exist. There is as yet no evidence that gas ammunition is available for the heavy projector (*see* p. 25, above), but the weapon might be used for putting up a concentration of gas.

iii. *Bulk contamination.*—Contamination batteries (*see* p. 9, above) are equipped with light and medium bulk contamination vehicles. These are standard light and medium semi-tracked vehicles on which containers have been mounted. The vehicles, therefore, resemble bulk petrol lorries, although the gas containers are much smaller in proportion to the vehicles they are mounted on. An inspection cover, pressure gauge, and control valves are fitted on the top rear of the container, together with what appears to be a spraying arm extending from the inspection cover well beyond the back of the vehicle. Emission is probably controlled from the driver's compartment.

Portable and hand sprayers are also envisaged.

3. *Gas in other arms*

i. *Artillery.*—The limitations of gas shell for artillery are clearly recognized. Nevertheless reports suggest that Germany continues to build up extensive stocks of gas charged shell.

It is the intention of the enemy to employ gas shell from both the light (10·5-cm.—4·14-in.) and heavy (15-cm.—5·91-in.) field howitzers. For types and markings of gas shell, *see* Table 9.

The difficulty of recognition will be increased by the fact that in all white, green, and blue ring charges, the projectile may contain an H.E. charge producing from 50–90 per cent. of the splintering effect of a similar projectile charged H.E. alone. There is no indication that the Germans have any airburst shell.

ii. *Infantry.*—It is intended to fire gas shell from both the light and the heavy *infantry guns*. For types and markings of infantry gas shells, *see* Table 9.

The following ammunition is known for the 8·1-cm. (3·16-in.) *mortar* :—

White ring.

It is, however, possible that any of the markings shown in Table 9 may be available.

iii. *Tank units.*—It is possible that tanks and armoured cars may be equipped with apparatus for spraying gas.

iv. *Engineers.—See* above, p. 13. No special equipment will be issued to engineers or infantry pioneers.

v. *Aircraft* :—

(a) *Aerial spray.*—Considerable research has been carried out on spray from aircraft and the Germans undoubtedly regard *low spray* (below 1,000 feet) as an effective weapon both against personnel and for ground contamination.

The various smoke-producing installations described on p. 27 above, are equally suitable for aerial gas spray. Chargings will probably be mustard gas, but lewisite and mixtures of mustard gas and lewisite have also been mentioned.

(b) *Aircraft bombs.*—Although information is scarce, there can be little doubt that much attention has been paid to the subject of gas bombs.

Bombs of the following sizes have been described : 10 kg. (22 lb.), 50 kg. (110 lb.), 250 kg (550 lb.), 500 kg. (1,100 lb.).*

It is reported that gas bombs will be of the following types :—

i. Gas bombs.—Yellow, green, blue, and white cross bombs containing 60 per cent. gas content, and fired by a percussion fuze and small bursting charge.

ii. HE/gas bombs.—Green cross, blue cross, and white cross bombs having a small gas content and fired by a percussion fuze. Besides the gas effect there is considerable fragmentation.

iii. Yellow cross spray bombs—with 60 per cent. gas content. A time fuze operates the bomb about 300 feet above the ground.

---

* It is not clear whether these figures refer to the actual weights of the bombs, or whether these are of the same dimensions as the corresponding H.E. bombs (i.e. considerably less than the indicated weight). Oil-filled incendiary bombs are of less weight than H.E. bombs of corresponding dimensions.

There have been several reports concerning the intended use of glass bombs to disperse gas, the containers varying from small sealed tubes to large cylinders, 6 feet in length. There is probably no technical difficulty in their manufacture and filling, but their fragile nature would render storage, transit, and use a hazardous matter.

4. Miscellaneous gas weapons

i. *Grenades.*—Although, no doubt, experiments have been carried out with these weapons, few details are available.

There have been reports that parachute troops are trained in the use of grenades charged with gas.

ii. *Lachrymatory bullets.*—The ammunition for the models 38 and 39 anti-tank rifle (Notes on the German Army—War, page 57) includes an A.P. tracer lachrymatory type, known as the Smk.H. Rs L'spur. This ammunition has a tungsten carbide core. 0·4 grain of C.A.P. is housed in a cavity in the base of the core in front of the tracer pellet.

iii. *Toxic generators.*—No evidence has been obtained that the Germans possess an official design of thermal toxic generator for offensive use, but should they wish to include such a weapon among their C.W. equipment they have ample material upon which to base their designs.

A private firm, Stoltzenberg, have manufactured generators containing D.A., D.C., and diphenylarsenic acid, which have been found to work very effectively, though their storage properties were not good.

The French had a large number of arsenical smoke generators which are now presumed to be in German hands. These are large, contain D.M., and discharge for about eight minutes. They are intended to be used in groups of four arranged to discharge one after the other, to give a total period of emission of about 30 minutes.

ADDENDUM

While this Note was in the press, further information has become available, of which the following is a summary :—

1. *Ref. Sec. 4, paras. 1 to 3*

i. In November 1941 new establishments were issued for the smoke troops. It is not believed that the basic organization has been altered, but many of the units have been renamed ; it is, however, to be expected that the old names will still be encountered.

The smoke regiment and battery are now to be called the *Werferregiment* and *Werferabteilung.* The regiment and battery of smoke mortar d have been replaced by the *schweres Werferregiment* and *schwere Werferabteilung*, for which the most convenient rendering is, heavy smoke regiment and battery (though it must be emphasized that the regiment fires more H.E. than smoke). There are still six smoke mortars d in a troop of smoke mortar d (*Werferbatterie 15-cm. Werfer* 41) : it is to be expected that troops of the two new rocket weapons (para. 2, i, below) will be included in some regiments.

ii. A new unit has also been identified, the mountain smoke battery (*Gebirgs-Nebelwerferabteilung*). Its organization is believed to be on the same lines as that of the normal smoke battery, but since the troops carry out only 40 per cent. smoke'ammunition and 60 per cent. H.E., its employment must be primarily as a mortar unit to fire H.E.

2. *Ref. Sec.* 10, *para.* 3, ii

i. Two new rocket weapons have now been identified. The 21-cm. (8·26-in.) *smoke mortar e* is probably a larger version of the 15-cm. (5·91-in.) smoke mortar d : only H.E. ammunition seems to be available. The 28/32-cm. (11/12·6-in.) *smoke mortar* fires the same ammunition as the heavy projector ; it probably works on the principle of the smoke mortar d, with an arrangement of six barrels. It is now known that a steel-frame version of the heavy projector exists.

ii. Rocket weapons have now been renamed as follows :—

	Old name	New name
Smoke mortar d	*Nebelwerfer d*	15-cm. *Nebelwerfer* 41 (or *Werfer* 41)
Smoke mortar e	*Nebelwerfer e*	21-cm. *Nebelwerfer* 42
28/32-cm. smoke mortar	—	28/32-cm. *Nebelwerfer* 41
Heavy projector (wooden frame)	*schweres Wurfgerät* 40	*schweres Wurfgerät* 40
Heavy projector (steel frame)	—	*schweres Wurfgerät* 41
Heavy projector (on armd. vehicle)	—	*schwerer Wurfrahmen* 40

The names given in the left-hand column are still the most convenient renderings.

NEW NOTES
ON THE
GERMAN ARMY

No 3

ENGINEERS

NOT TO BE PUBLISHED

The information given in this document is not to be communicated, either directly or indirectly, to the Press or any person not holding an official position in His Majesty's Service.

Crown Copyright Reserved

Prepared under the direction of
The Chief of the Imperial General Staff

THE WAR OFFICE,
January, 1943

This document must not fall into enemy hands

26/G.S. Publications/886

DISTRIBUTION

All arms	Scale A
G.H.Q., Home Forces	10 copies
Command H.Q. (including A.A.)	5 ,,
London and Northern Ireland districts	5 ,,
Corps H.Q. (including A.A.)	4 ,,
Divisional H.Q. (including A.A.)	3 ,,
Brigade H.Q. (including A.A.)	2 ,,
All group H.Qs.	2 ,,
H.Q., areas, districts, garrisons, sub-areas	1 copy
Intelligence training centre	150 copies
Intelligence training centre (Cambridge Wing)	50 ,,

CONTENTS

	PAGE
Preface	1
Introduction	2

PART I.—ORGANIZATION

A.—INFANTRY PIONEERS AND DIVISIONAL ENGINEERS

SEC.
1. Infantry pioneer platoons ... 4
2. Divisional engineer battalions ... 7

B.—UNITS IN THE G.H.Q. POOL

3. Engineer regiments and battalions ... 21
4. Bridging and assault boat units ... 22
5. Obstacle units ... 23
6. Parks ... 23
7. Railway engineers ... 24
8. Fortress engineers ... 25
9. Technical troops ... 26
10. Construction units ... 27
11. Siebel ferry units ... 28

PART II—EQUIPMENT

12. Bridging equipment ... 29
13. Electrical and mechanical equipment ... 32
14. Anti-tank and anti-personnel obstacles ... 32
15. Mines and mine detectors ... 34
16. Demolition equipment ... 35
17. Flame throwers ... 37
18. Landing craft ... 39

Appendix 1. Assault detachments ... 39
Appendix 2. Spigot mortars ... 40

TABLES

		PAGE
1.	Infantry pioneer platoons—strength and equipment	6
2.	Engineer battalion in an infantry division—organization ...	8
3.	Mountain engineer battalion in a mountain division—organization ...	9
4.	Mechanized engineer battalion in a motorized division—organization ...	10
5.	Armoured engineer battalion in an armoured division—organization ...	11
6.	Engineer battalion in an infantry division—strength and equipment ...	12
7.	Mountain engineer battalion in a mountain division—strength and equipment ...	14
8.	Mechanized engineer battalion in a motorized division—strength and equipment ...	16
9.	Armoured engineer battalion in an armoured division—strength and equipment ...	18
10.	Armoured engineer company—strength and firepower ...	20
11.	Flame throwers ...	38

PREFACE

The following paragraph, chapter and appendices of Notes on the German Army—War are superseded by the present New Note :—

Chapter III, para. 12 (a).
Chapter VIII.
Appendix XXVI.
Appendix XXVII.

INTRODUCTION

1. Notes on the German Army—War gives the organization and equipment of German engineer units according to information received up to the end of the Battle of France. It is now possible to give a much fuller picture, mainly from documents and equipment captured in the Middle East.

2. The units included in the present New Note are classified by the Germans as follows :—

(a) Infantry pioneers (*Infanteriepioniere*, or *Truppenpioniere*) (Sec. **1**).

These are infantry personnel with some engineer training; they wear the distinguishing colour of their own arm (infantry, mountain infantry, etc.).

(b) Engineers, including bridgebuilding battalions (Secs. **2–6**).

Railway engineers, including railway construction battalions (Sec. **7**).

Fortress engineers, including fortress construction battalions (Sec. **8**).

Technical troops (Sec. **9**).

These wear black as their distinguishing colour, and the official designation of the other ranks is *Pionier*.

(c) Construction troops (*Bautruppen*) (Sec. **10**).

These wear light brown as their distinguishing colour, and the official designation of the other ranks is *Bausoldat*.

3. On the Army General Staff (*Generalstab des Heeres*, see The German Forces in the Field, 1942, A4), the General of Engineers and Fortresses, General Jacob, who is also Inspector of Fortresses, is adviser on all questions of policy affecting engineers and construction troops, and is also responsible for the welfare of all G.H.Q. engineers and construction troops. In the General Army Branch of the War Office (The German Forces in the Field, 1942, A6) the training and equipment of these units is divided as follows between the inspectorates :—

Inspectorate 5—Engineers.

Inspectorate of Fortresses—Fortress engineers and construction troops.

(These two inspectorates are very closely connected.

Inspectorate 10—Railway engineers.

Inspectorate 11—Technical troops.

In the Army Ordnance Branch of the War Office, engineer and fortress equipment is dealt with by the branches abbreviated *Wa Prüf* 5 and *Wa I Rü* 5.

In the field, there is a General of Engineers at Army Group H.Q., and an Army Engineer Commander (*Armee-Pionierführer*) at Army H.Q. At Division, the commander of the divisional engineer battalion advises the divisional commander on engineer matters.

4. The distinction between engineers and construction units lies in their employment rather than in their organization. German engineers pride themselves on being fighting troops; the substance of the boast is largely that non-technical and less combatant duties are assigned to construction troops, who are regarded as a separate arm, or else to para-military bodies like the *Organisation Todt*. It may, however, be noted that in 1941 it was decided that construction units and fortress engineers, should be fully armed with rifles (previously about 50 per cent. had rifles).

PART I.—ORGANIZATION

A.—INFANTRY PIONEERS AND DIVISIONAL ENGINEERS

1. Infantry pioneer platoons

1. Infantry pioneer platoons are composed of infantry personnel with engineer training. Their infantry training lays particular stress on close fighting, use of smoke grenades, use of explosives, and assault operations against fixed defences and strongpoints—in fact, on the role they are to play in assault detachments (Appendix 1). Their engineer training covers thoroughly the use of the equipment allotted to them (Table 1). They are to be capable of carrying out most kinds of minor engineer tasks, but it is emphasized that they must not be used on tasks for which divisional engineers are better equipped. For their possible role in chemical warfare, see New Notes No. 2, p. 13,

2. Their distribution is as follows:—

(a) *Infantry divisions.*—The regimental H.Q. company of every infantry regiment contains an infantry pioneer platoon (*Infanterie-Pionierzug*). It consists of H.Q., six sections, and horse-drawn transport. Groups of two sections each may be allotted to battalions: the transport of the platoon is so loaded that it can also readily operate in two groups of three sections each. There is no pioneer platoon in the normal infantry battalion.

(b) *Mountain divisions.*—A mountain pioneer platoon (*Gebirgsjäger-Pionierzug*) is included in the heavy company of every mountain infantry battalion (5th, 10th, or 15th company of the regiment). The platoon consists of H.Q., three sections, and pack transport. The H.Q. company of the mountain infantry regiment probably has a similar platoon.

(c) *Motorized and armoured divisions.*—Mechanized pioneer platoons (*Pionierzug motorisiert*) of a standard pattern are included in the following:—

    i. H.Q. company of Panzer grenadier regiments (except where this platoon has now been replaced by an anti-tank platoon);

    ii. Heavy company of Panzer grenadier and motor-cycle battalions;

iii. Heavy squadron of mechanized reconnaissance units (in such divisions as still have these units).

The pioneer platoons of the following are also mechanized and probably follow the same pattern :—

iv. H.Q. company of motorized infantry regiments ;
v. H.Q. squadron of tank battalions.

The mechanized pioneer platoon consists of H.Q., three sections, and motor transport.

3. Personnel and equipment of pioneer platoons are given in Table 1. The establishment of the mechanized pioneer platoon was increased in 1941 to include new personnel for bridging operations. The platoon has now *either* D bridging equipment (Sec. **12,** para. 4 (*b*) below) *or* material for improvised bridging. The latter appears to be a standard set of equipment; no details are available, but *see* Sec. **12,** para. 6. The former was earlier allotted only to the pioneer platoons of mechanized reconnaissance units, presumably for their armoured cars ; the extension to Panzer grenadier regiments is no doubt due to the increasing allotment of armoured troop-carriers.

At the same time the quantity of demolition stores carried was increased, and the quantity of hand-grenades, wire-cutters, etc., cut down. It is evidently intended that the mechanized pioneer platoon shall perform a more strictly engineering role than before. It is not likely that any similar development has taken place in non-mechanized pioneer platoons.

TABLE 1
INFANTRY PIONEER PLATOONS—STRENGTH AND EQUIPMENT

(a) Personnel, weapons, etc.

	Personnel			H.T.		M.T.		L.M.G.	Hand grenades	Smoke grenades	Smoke generators	Wire cutters
	Officers	O.Rs.	Total	Horses (or pack animals)	Horsedrawn vehicles	Motor vehicles	M.C.					
Inf. pnr. pl. ...	1	76	77	11	5	—	—	3	60	15	—	12
Mtn. pnr. pl. ...	1	34	35	11	—	—	—	3	60	—	—	—
Mech. pnr. pl. ...	1	60	61	—	—	11	4	3	30	15	48	6

(b) Engineer equipment.

	Small pneumatic boats	Large pneumatic boats	Power saws	Plain wire (concertina rolls)	Mine detectors	Demolition stores, lbs.	Exploders	Instantaneous fuze, yds.	Sandbags
Inf. pnr. pl. ...	9	—	—	—	4	172	—	164	60
Mtn. pnr. pl. ...	2	—	—	—	4	411	2	109	15
Mech. pnr. pl. ...	5	5	1	24	3	397	—	327	50

2. Divisional engineer battalions

1. For the organization of engineer battalions in infantry, mountain, motorized, and armoured divisions, *see* Tables 2–5 For their equipment, *see* Tables 6–9.

2. All companies, except the armoured engineer company, contain three identical platoons of three sections each. The organization of the armoured engineer company is given in Table 5, details of personnel, etc., in Table 10.

Bridging columns have normally two identical platoons (*Pontonzüge*) to carry the main pontoon and trestle equipment, and a third platoon (*Ergänzungszug*) with supplementary equipment. Where there is a tank bridgelaying platoon, this is the third platoon, and the supplementary equipment platoon becomes the fourth platoon.

The light engineer column combines the functions of the E. & M. Tools Park and the Reserve Store Park, given in " Notes on the German Army—War," p. 127, etc.

TABLE 2.
ENGINEER BATTALION IN AN INFANTRY DIVISION.—ORGANIZATION

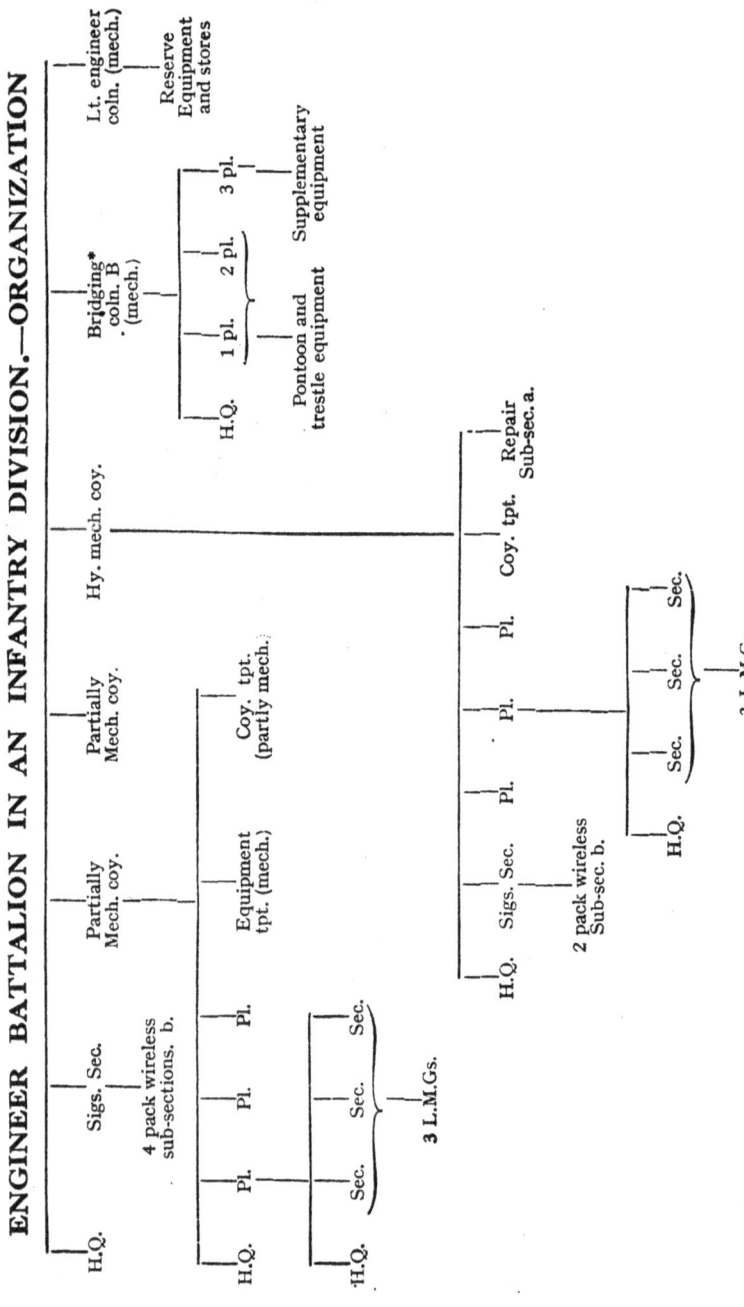

* In place of Br. coln. B, some battalions probably still have a Br. coln. C (Sec. 12, para. 3, b).

TABLE 3
MOUNTAIN ENGINEER BATTALION IN A MOUNTAIN DIVISION—ORGANIZATION

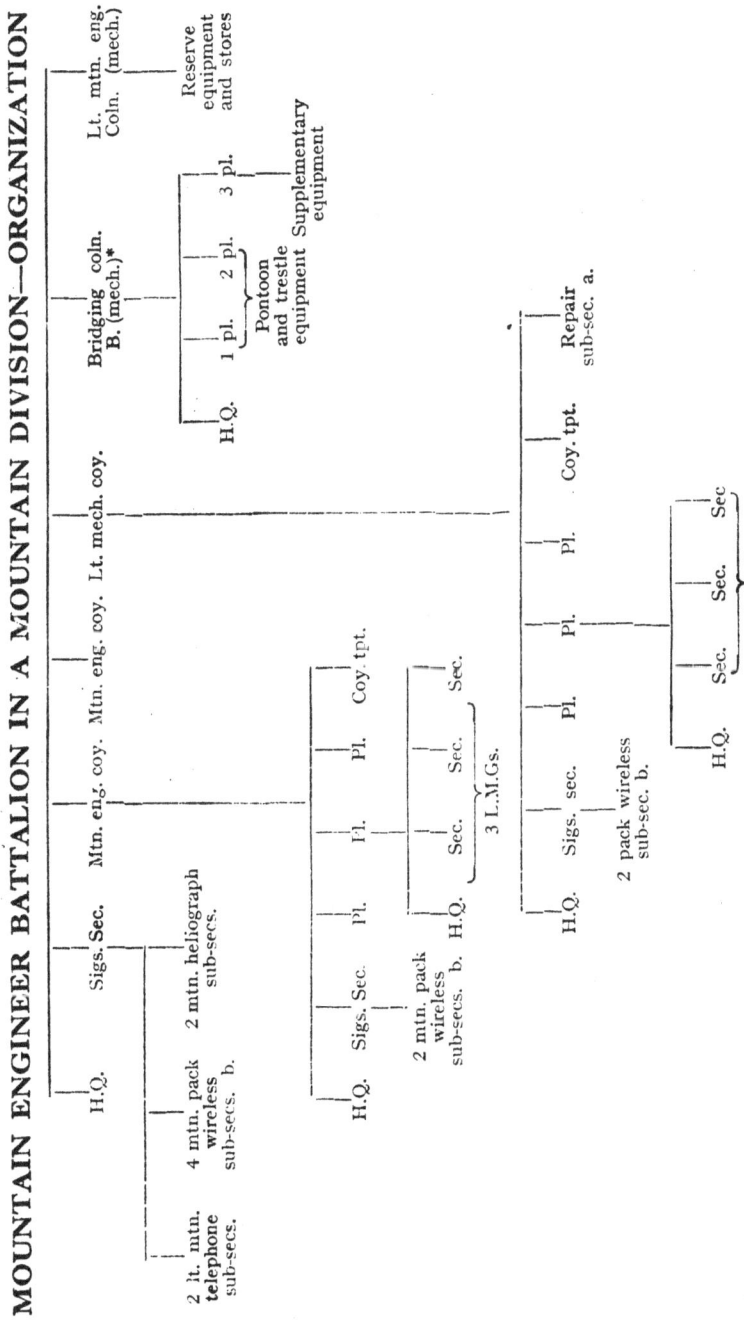

* Attached when necessary.

TABLE 4
MECHANIZED ENGINEER BATTALION IN A MOTORIZED INFANTRY DIVISION—ORGANIZATION

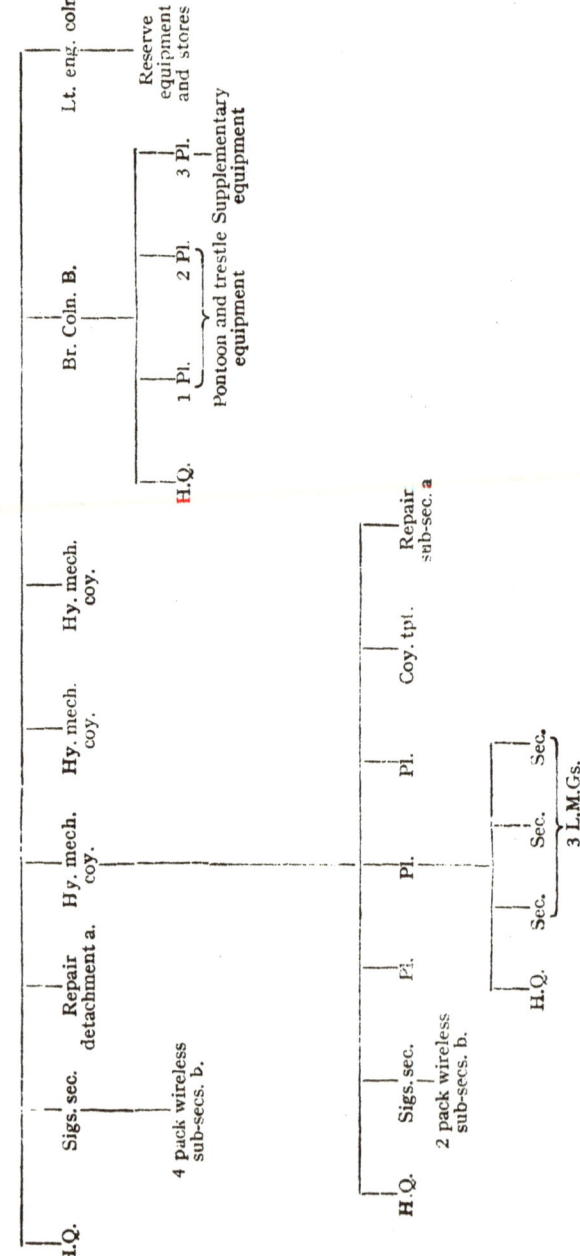

TABLE 5.
ARMOURED ENGINEER BATTALION IN AN ARMOURED DIVISION—ORGANIZATION

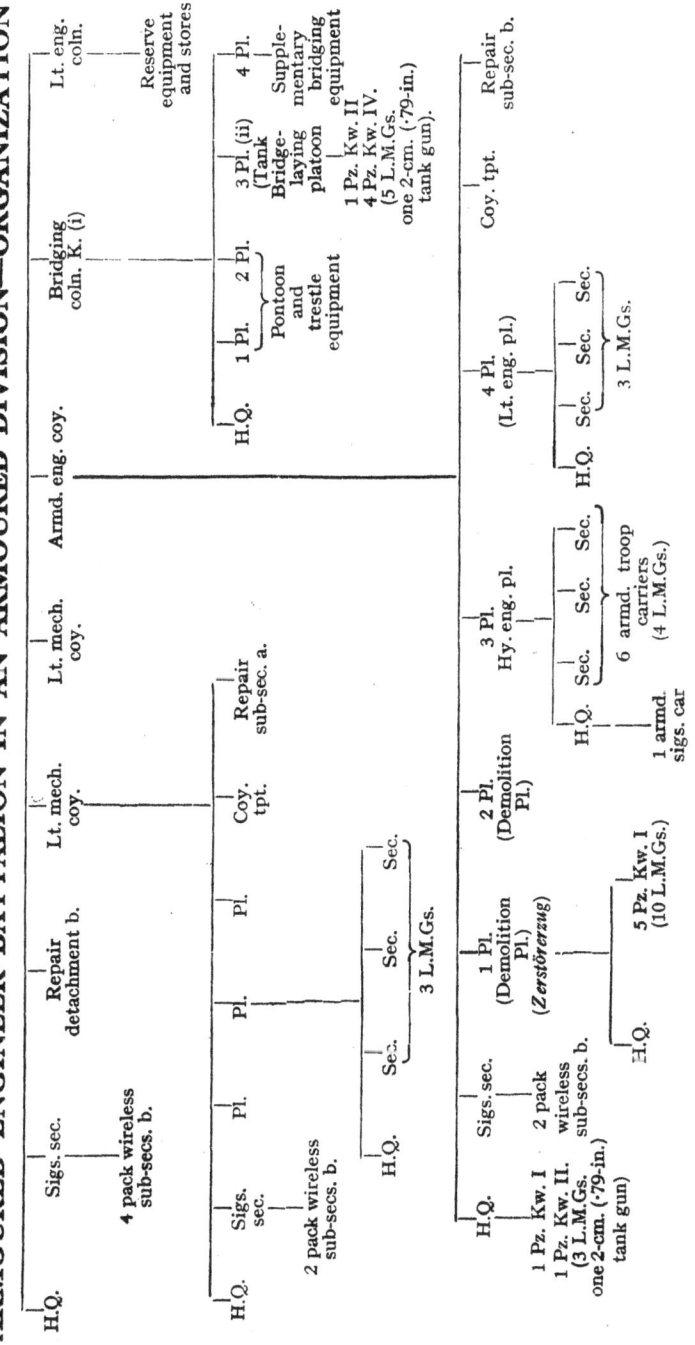

NOTES

(i) In place of Br. Coln. K some battalions may still have Br. Coln. B (tables 2 and 6). Some armoured divisions have now two bridging columns, either two K, or one B and one K.
(ii) It is not known in how many battalions a tank bridge-laying platoon has as yet been formed. The nature of the bridge-laying equipment is not known.

TABLE 6
ENGINEER BATTALION IN AN INFANTRY DIVISION.
STRENGTH AND EQUIPMENT

(a) *Personnel, weapons, etc.*

	Personnel			H.T.		M.T.		L.M.G.	Hand grenades	Smoke generators	Small flame throwers	Medium flame throwers
	Officers	O.Rs.	Total	Horses	Horse-drawn vehicles	Motor vehicles	M.C.					
Bn. H.Q.	5	36	41	10	3	3	7	—	—	—	—	—
Partly mech. coy. (2) ...	4	187	191	21	8	6	5	9	190	156	—	—
Hy. mech. coy.	4	203	207	—	—	21	12	9	190	156	—	—
Br. coln. B (i)	2	100	102	—	—	35	7	—	—	—	—	—
Lt. eng. coln.	3	65	68	—	—	16	7	—	480	324	6	3
Total	22	778	800	52	19	87	43	27	1050 (ii)	792	6	3

(b) *Engineer equipment*

	Small pneumatic boats	Large pneumatic boats	16-ton ramps	Small compressors	Large compressors	Drilling equipment, sets	Power saws	Welding equipment, sets	Plain wire (concertina rolls)	Barbed wire (concertina rolls)	Tellermines	S-mines	Mine detectors	Demolition stores, lb.	Exploders	Instantaneous fuze, yds.	Hand searchlights	Sandbags
Partly mech. coy. (2) ...	6	4	—	—	2	2	6	2	42	—	40	—	10	1053	6	327	—	200
Hy. mech. coy. ...	4	3	—	3	—	3	9	—	76	—	296	—	10	2091	9	654	—	600
Br. coln. B (i) ...	48	24	8	—	—	—	—	—	12	—	—	—	—	—	—	—	—	—
Lt. eng. coln. ...	—	—	—	—	2	2	2	3	100	66	600	621	—	2788	2	1635	10	600
Total ...	64	35	8	3	6	9	23	7	272	66	976 (ii)	621 (ii)	30	6985 (ii)	23	2943	10	1600

NOTES.—(i) Some engineer battalions still have bridging column C, with a smaller establishment.
    (ii) In addition, divisional supply columns carry the following :—
        3,525 hand grenades, of which 375 are for the engineer battalion.
        800 Tellermines.
        801 S-mines.
        5,180 lb. demolition stores.

TABLE 7
MOUNTAIN ENGINEER BATTALION IN A MOUNTAIN DIVISION. STRENGTH AND EQUIPMENT

(a) *Personnel, weapons, etc.*

	Personnel			H.T.		M.T.		L.M.G.	Hand grenades	Smoke generators	Small flame throwers	Medium flame throwers
	Officers	O.Rs.	Total	Horses and pack animals	Horse-drawn vehicles	Motor vehicles	M.C.					
Bn. H.Q.	7	106	113	44	8	4	7	—	—	—	—	—
Mtn. eng. coy. (2) ...	4	273	277	106	28	1	2	9	190	156	—	—
Lt. mech. coy. ...	4	206	210	—	—	35	18	9	190	156	—	—
Lt. mtn. eng. coln. ...	2	68	70	—	—	20	7	—	480	324	6	3
TOTAL ...	21	926	947	256	64	61	36	27	1,050 (ii)	792	6	3
Br. coln. B (i) ...	2	100	102	—	—	35	7	—	—	—	—	—
Total with br. coln.B. ...	23	1,026	1,049	256	64	96	43	27	1,050 (ii)	792	6	3

(b) Engineer Equipment

	Small pneumatic boats	Large pneumatic boats	16-ton ramps	Small compressors	Large compressors	Drilling equipment, sets	Power saws	Welding equipment, sets	Plain wire (concertina rolls)	Barbed wire (concertina rolls)	Barbed wire (50-lb. coils)	Tellermines	S-Mines	Mine detectors	Demolition stores, lb.	Exploders	Instantaneous fuze, yds.	Hand searchlights	Sand bags
Mtg. eng. coy. (2) ...	6	2		3		3	6	1	42		16	40		10	1,059	6	327		200
Lt. mech. coy. ...	4	3		3		3	9		94			308		10	2,383	9	817		675
Lt. mtn. eng. coln. ...					2	2	2	3	100	66		300	387		2,788	2	1,635	10	600
TOTAL ...	16	7		9	2	11	23	5	278	66	32	688 (ii)	387 (ii)	30	7,277 (ii)	23	3,106	10	1,675
Br. coln. B (i) ...	48	24	8						12										
Total with br. coln. B.	64	31	8	9	2	11	23	5	290	66	32	688 (ii)	387 (ii)	30	7,277 (ii)	23	3,106	10	1,675

NOTES.— (i) Attached when necessary.
(ii) In addition, divisional supply columns carry the following :—
    3,525 hand grenades, of which 375 are for the engineer battalion.
    800 Tellermines.
    801 S-Mines.
    5,180 lb. demolition stores.

TABLE 8

MECHANIZED ENGINEER BATTALION IN A MOTORIZED INFANTRY DIVISION. STRENGTH AND EQUIPMENT

(a) Personnel, weapons, etc.

	Personnel			MT.						
	Officers	O.Rs.	Total	Motor vehicles	M.C.	L.M.G.	Hand grenades	Smoke generators	Small flame throwers	Large flame throwers
Bn. H.Q.	7	64	71	19	9	—	—	—	—	—
Hy. mech. coy. (3) ...	4	203	207	21	12	9	190	156	—	—
Br. coln. B	2	100	102	35	7	—	—	—	—	—
Lt. eng. coln.	3	65	68	16	7	—	480	324	6	3
Total	24	838	862	133	59	27	1050 (i)	792	6	3

(b) *Engineer equipment*

	Small pneumatic boats	Large pneumatic boats	16-ton ramps	Small compressors	Large compressors	Drilling equipment, sets	Power saws	Welding equipment, sets	Plain wire (concertina rolls)	Barbed wire (concertina rolls)	Tellermines	S-mines	Mine detectors	Demolition stores, lb.	Exploders	Instantaneous fuze, yds.	Hand searchlights	Sandbags
Hy. mech. coy. (3) ...	4	3	—	3	—	3	9	—	—	—	296	—	10	2091	9	654	—	600
Br. coln. B. ...	48	24	8	—	—	—	—	—	12	—	—	—	—	—	—	—	—	—
Lt. eng. coln ...	—	—	—	—	2	2	2	3	100	66	600	621	—	2788	2	1635	10	600
Total ...	60	33	8	9	2	11	29	3	340	66	1488 (i)	621 (i)	30	9061 (i)	29	3597	10	2400

NOTES.—(i) In addition, divisional supply columns carry the following :—
3,525 hand grenades, of which 375 are for the engineer battalion.
800 Tellermines
801 S-mines.
5,180 lb. demolition stores.

TABLE 9
ARMOURED ENGINEER BATTALION IN AN ARMOURED DIVISION. STRENGTH AND EQUIPMENT

(a) *Personnel, weapons, etc.*

	Personnel			Tanks			Armd. vehs.		M.T.								
	Officers	O.Rs.	Total	Pz. Kw. I	Pz. Kw. II	Pz. Kw. IV (Bridge laying)	Armd. Sigs. Car	Armd. Troop Carriers	Motor vehicles	M.C.	L.M.G.	2-cm. (.79-in.) tank guns	Hand grenades	Smoke grenades	Smoke generators	Small flame throwers	Medium flame throwers
Bn. H.Q.	7	64	71	—	—	—	—	—	19	9	—	—	—	—	—	—	—
Lt. mech. coy. (2) ...	4	206	210	—	—	—	—	—	35	18	9	—	190	—	156	—	—
Armd. eng. coy (i) ...	5	198	203	11	1	—	1	6	26	15	35	1	450	90	144	—	—
Br. coln. K. (ii) without tank bridge-laying pl. ...	2	96	98	—	—	—	—	—	37	9	—	—	—	—	—	—	—
Tank bridge-laying pl.	1	21	22	—	1	4	—	—	1	1	5	1	—	—	—	—	—
Lt. eng. coln.	3	60	63	—	—	—	—	—	19	7	—	—	600	225	108	6	3
Total	26	851	877	11	2	4	1	6	172	77	58	2	1,430 (iii)	315	564	6	3

(a) *Engineer equipment*

	Small pneumatic boats	Large pneumatic boats	16-ton ramps	Small compressors	Large compressors	Drilling equipment, sets	Power saws	Welding equipment, sets	Plain wire (concertina rolls)	Barbed wire (concertina rolls)	Tellermines	S-mines	Mine detectors	Demolition stores, lb.	Exploders	Instantaneous fuze, yds.	Hand searchlights	Sand bags
Lt. mech. coy. (2) ...	4	3	—	3	—	3	9	—	94	—	308	—	10	2,383	9	817	—	675
Armd. eng. coy. ...	2	2	12	1	—	1	3	—	54	—	188	—	10	7,065	6	654	—	625
Br. Coln. K (ii) without tank bridge-laying pl. ...	24	16	64	—	—	—	—	—	12	—	—	—	—	—	—	—	—	—
Lt. eng. coln. ...	—	—	—	—	1	3	2	2	90	60	450	450	—	4,538	2	1,635	5	1,200
Total ...	34	24	76	7	1	10	23	2	344	60	1,254 (iii)	450 (iii)	30	16,369 (iii)	26	3,923	5	3,175

NOTES.—
(i) *See* table 10 and notes.
(ii) Some armoured divisions may still have bridging column B, *see* tables 6–8, though bridging column K is now standard for armoured divisions. Some divisions have two columns, either two K, or one B and one K. It is not known what engineer equipment is carried by the tank bridge-laying platoon.
(iii) In addition, divisional supply columns carry the following :—
    3,525 Land grenades, of which 375 are for the engineer battalion.
    800 Tellermines.
    801 S-mines.
    5,186 lb. demolition stores.

TABLE 10

ARMOURED ENGINEER COMPANY—STRENGTH AND FIRE POWER

	Personnel			Tanks		Armd. vehicles		M.T.			
	Officers	O.Rs.	Total	Pz. Kw. I	Pz. Kw. II	Armd. Sigs. Cars	Armd. Troop carriers	Motor vehicles	M.C.	L.M.G.	2-cm. (·79-in.) tank guns
H.Q.	1	12	13	1	1	—	—	1	3	3	1
Sigs. sec.	—	6	6	—	—	—	—	2	—	—	—
1 and 2 (demolition) pls. (each) ...	1	17	18	5	—	—	—	1	1	10	—
3 (hy. eng.) ...	1	52	53	—	—	1	6	1	2	4	—
4 (lt. eng.) pl. ...	1	56	57	—	—	—	—	8	2	8	—
Repair sub-sec. b.	—	9	9	—	—	—	—	2	2	—	—
Coy. tpt.	—	29	29	—	—	—	—	10	4	—	—
Total ...	5	198	203	11	1	1	6	26	15	35	1

NOTE.—The armoured engineer company's organization varies with the equipment available :—
  (a) Where no Pz. Kw. I are available, 1 and 2 platoons are replaced by a single light engineer platoon.
  (b) Where no armoured troop-carriers are available 3 platoon is organized as a light engineer platoon.
  (c) For the possible allotment of armoured troop-carriers fitted to fire the ammunition of the heavy projector, see New Notes No. 2, p. 9.

B.—UNITS IN THE G.H.Q. POOL

3. Engineer regiments and battalions

1. There is no standard allotment of engineer units to German corps or armies. All engineer units outside divisions belong to the G.H.Q. pool, and are allotted to corps or armies as needed. Where they are not engaged in active operations there will normally be no allotment, except on a small scale for training. For active operations, the allotment is usually generous.

Each army has, however, its own army engineer park (*Armeepionierpark*, Sec. **6**).

2. *Regiment and battalion staffs.*—There are no regularly constituted engineer regiments, except in the railway engineers (Sec. **7**). There are, however, certain regimental staffs, which may be allotted to corps or armies to control the G.H.Q. engineer units allotted to them. They consist of H.Q., signal section, and transport; strength is as follows:—

	Officers	O.Rs.	Total	Motor vehicles	M.C.
H.Q. and transport	4	34	38	7	9
Sigs. sec. ...	1	31	32	7	1
Total ...	5	65	70	14	10

Special battalion staffs (*Stab Pionierbataillons z. b. V.*), with similar functions, also exist.

3. *G.H.Q. engineer battalions.*—So far as is known, these are organized on the same lines as the divisional engineer battalions and consist of H.Q. with signal section, three companies, a bridging column, and a light engineer column. The companies are probably in most cases heavy mechanized companies, and the strength of the battalion will be roughly the same as that of the engineer battalion in a motorized division (Tables 4 and 8).

The names "corps engineer battalion" and "army engineer battalion" may still be encountered, but the use of these names will be due either to the past history or the present allocation of the unit. Certain battalions had at one time three bridging columns, but it is believed that in all cases two of these columns have now been detached permanently for use as independent bridging columns (Sec. **4,** para. 1).

4. *Engineer demonstrational unit (Pionier-Lehrbataillon).—* Units of this type, like the demonstrational units of other arms, may be encountered in the field. Their composition is variable : one such unit is known to have included, as a fourth company, an assault boat company (Sec. **4,** para. 3). Some units specialize in particular kinds of equipment : there is for instance an *engineer demonstrational unit for heavy bridgebuilding.*

4. Bridging and assault boat units

1. *G.H.Q. bridging columns.*—These are mostly bridging columns B, as in the infantry or motorized division (Tables 2, 4, 6, 8). Columns with other equipment may also occur. Carrying units for heavier bridges are usually referred to as " units " of the equipment concerned, e.g. *Einheit leichtes Brückengerät, Einheit Herbertgerät,* etc. These units are sometimes under control of a special battalion staff (*Stab Transportabteilung für schweres Brückengerät*).

For active operations, the allotment of bridging columns is lavish ; for instance, one corps in Russia had seven, in addition to the column of a G.H.Q. engineer battalion also attached to it.

2. *Bridge-building battalions (Brückenbaubataillone).*—Bridging columns are purely carrying units, and the bridges are erected either by the personnel of an engineer battalion, or by special bridge-building battalions. These consist of H.Q., four companies, an engineer tools platoon (Sec. **6,** paras. 2 and 3), and an engineer park company. The strength of the company is about 250 all ranks, and the total battalion strength will be approximately 1,250.

3. *Assault boat companies and detachments (Sturmbootkompanien, -kommandos).*—An assault boat company consists of H.Q. with signals section, and 3 platoons of 3 sections each. The total establishment strength is 194 all ranks, with 4 L.M.G. and 3 anti-tank rifles, and an unspecified quantity of Tellermines and demolition stores ; 36 assault boats are carried.

Recent practice, however, appears to be to make up assault boat detachments of varying size for service where required : the most usual type has three platoons with 81 assault boats in all.

4. *Assault engineer companies (Sturmpionierkompanien).*—
The strength of these companies appears to be about 200.
The company contains two platoons of engineers trained in
assault operations, and a third assault boat platoon with 27
assault boats.

5. Obstacle units

1. Certain companies (*Pionier-Sperrkompanien*) and carrying units (*Pionier-Sperrkolonnen*) specialize in anti-tank obstacles. (These units appear to have been used operationally as late as 1940, but the company may by now be obsolete.) The strength of the company is not known, but it carries about 250 Tellermines in addition to other equipment. The carrying unit has 1 officer and 53 O.Rs., 20 motor vehicles, and 4 motor cycles; it carries 270 concertina rolls of plain wire, 3,000 Tellermines, 4,230 lb. demolition equipment and 2,250 yards instantaneous fuze.

6. Parks

1. One engineer park is allotted to each army. No recent information is available, but the following pre-war data are given as an indication of the unit's function.

2. Organization was as follows :—

   (a) The engineer park itself, divided into H.Q., a section for roadmaking equipment, and a section for other equipment.

   (b) Two engineer park companies, sub-divisions unknown; they are intended for maintenance and repair.

   (c) An engineer tools platoon (*Pionier-Maschinenzug*), divided into two half-platoons and a workshop section.

3. Strength was as follows :—

	Officers	O.Rs.	Total	Motor Vehicles	Trailers (various)	M.C.
Engineer park	4	70	74	9	12	3
Eng. Pk. Coy. (each)	3	190	193	—	—	1
Eng. Tools Pl.	1	102	103	26	19	4
Total	11	552	563	35	31	9

4. Holdings included the following :—
   ½ set each of B and C bridging equipment, with 25 vehicles (the proportion of C equipment would now be lower).
   1 L.Z. bridge (Sec. **12**, para. 5a).
   8 sets of road-making equipment.
   8 sets of equipment for repair of concrete roads.
   2 sets of equipment for repair of macadam roads.

Details of these last three items are not available, but the total roadmaking equipment is stated to be enough to employ 4,280 men, i.e. some three road construction battalions (Sec. **10**, para. 2).

5. There are also static *home engineer parks* (*Heimatpionierpark*) in every military district (*Wehrkreis*) in Germany, with larger holdings.

7. Railway engineers

1. These belong to the engineer arm, and are to be regarded as fighting troops in the same sense as other engineer units. Certain classes of the original personnel were drawn from the German state railways, but present replacements are almost entirely from railway engineer depot units of the army. They are mainly employed on railway construction and maintenance in the forward areas, though some units are certainly concerned in railway operation as well. A large part of their duty is the construction of bridges heavier than the K equipment, and they may be found erecting, e.g. the L.Z. bridge (Sec. **12**, para. 5a) for roads as well as railways.

2. *Railway engineer regiments* have two battalions of four companies each, the companies being numbered consecutively through the regiment. The companies may be partly or wholly mechanized. There is no indication of their strength, except that given in Sec. **12**, para. 5a. Mention has also been made of a *railway engineer brigade staff*, which may be used to control two or more regiments.

3. *Railway bridge building battalions* appear to be organized in the same way as bridge building battalions (Sec. **4**, para. 2), i.e. they contain four companies, a railway engineer tools platoon, and a railway park company. The carrying units of railway bridges (Sec. **12**, para. 5d) are also counted as railway engineers.

4. *Railway construction battalions* are also railway engineers. There are probably four companies to the battalion, but no details are available.

5. There are also the following specialist companies :—

(a) Independent *railway construction companies*.

(b) *Railway pier-building companies* (*Eisenbahn-Pfeilerbaukompanie*), for heavy bridges.

(c) *Railway telephone companies*.

(d) *Railway signalling companies* (*Eisenbahnstellwerkkompanie*).

(e) *Railway water-point companies* (*Eisenbahnwasserstationskompanie*).

(f) **Light railway companies** (*Feldbahnkompanie*).

(g) *Railway operating companies* (*Eisenbahnbetriebskompanie*).

(h) *Rope railway detachments and sections* (*Seilbahnkommando, -trupp*).

(i) *Underwater welding sections* (*Eisenbahnunterwasserschneidetrupp*).

The employment of these units can usually be guessed from their title, though it is not always clear whether they are concerned with construction, maintenance, or operation. The construction companies are by far the most numerous. The organization is less clear. *Railway engineer construction staffs* (*Eisenbahnpionieroberbaustab*) probably control the construction units.

6. *Railway engineer parks* and *railway engineer workshop companies* form part of the rearward organization of the railway engineers. These are controlled by a special railway engineer staff (*Eisenbahnpionierstab z.b.V.*) in Berlin.

7. The above units, which are railway engineer units, must be distinguished from units of the railway troops (*Eisenbahntruppen*), which are concerned with the maintenance and operation of railways in the rearward area and are not engineer units.

8. Fortress engineers

1. These are mainly specialists, and, except in theatres where their technical skill is required, are not likely to be encountered in the field.

2. The organization in outline is as follows :—Each military district (*Wehrkreis*) has a *fortress engineer* H.Q. (*Festungs-Pionier-Kommandeur*) ; under this are staffs equivalent to regimental staffs (*Festungs-Pionierstab*), of which each normally controls two *sector groups* (*Festungs-Pionierabschnittsgruppe*). There are also *fortress construction battalions, fortress engineer parks, fortress engineer supply staffs*, etc.

3. Certain specialist units of fortress engineers connected with water supply have been employed in Africa. Units of the following types are known :—

(a) Light and heavy water supply companies (*Kompanie Wasserversorgung*).

(b) Water distillation companies (*Kompanie Wasserdestillation*). These are employed in the distillation of fresh from salt water.

(c) Water purification columns (*Filterkolonne*).

4. Military geological stations (*Wehrgeologenstelle*) belonging to the fortress engineers have also been encountered.

9. Technical troops

1. These are industrial specialist units, belonging to the engineers, which appear to have been created at the end of 1940. They are organized in battalions, often of three companies (not necessarily of the same kind). They are primarily concerned in the initial exploitation of occupied countries, the reconstruction of damaged installations, etc., and work very far forward.

2. The following are known :—

(a) A staff equivalent to a regimental staff (*Kommandeur technischer Truppen*).

(b) *Technical battalions*, without qualification, controlling a mixture of companies.

(c) *Technical battalions for mineral oil* (*Mineralöl*). These may be for construction (*Bau*) or operation (*Betrieb*) of oil installations, and have been reported in Rumania and in Russia.

(d) *Electricity companies* (*technische Kompanie E*).

(e) *Gas and water companies* (*technische Kompanie GW*).

(f) *Mining companies* (*technische Kompanie BT*).—These may be either for underground mining (*Tiefbau*) or opencast mining (*Tagebau*).

The strength of these units is not known. The companies have usually 3 L.M.G. each and are evidently to be regarded as combatant units.

10. Construction units

1. These are not engineer units (though it is convenient to include them here), and are not in the same sense combatant troops. In 1941, it was, however, decided that construction units, and most fortress engineer units, should be fully armed with rifles.

Construction battalions (*Baubataillone*) come under the control of a staff equivalent to a regimental staff (*Kommandeur der Bautruppe*), which in its turn may be controlled by a higher construction staff (*Oberbaustab*). The battalion contains H.Q., four companies, and second line transport (*Baukolonne*); the transport may or may not be mechanized, but the companies are not. The strength of the company is about 400 all ranks; the whole battalion about 1900. Some companies are concrete construction companies (*Betonbaukompanie*), of about the same strength.

2. *Road construction battalions.*—These are of three types. The road construction battalion (*Strassenbaubataillon*) consists of H.Q., four road construction companies, and a partly mechanized equipment section. The companies contain H.Q. with signal section, three platoons, a mechanized equipment column, and horsedrawn transport. The company strength is about 360, the battalion total is about 1,500 all ranks.

The light road construction battalion (*leichtes Strassenbaubataillon*) has H.Q. and four light road construction companies, but has no equipment section. The companies are considerably smaller, and have no signal section; company strength is about 180, total battalion strength about 750.

The light cyclist road construction battalion (*leichtes Radfahr-Strassenbaubataillon*) contains four light cyclist road construction companies. Otherwise it is similar to the light road construction battalion.

Transport in these battalions is on a small scale, not enough to move the battalion and its equipment.

3. *Agricultural construction battalions* (*Landesbaubataillon*).—Little is known of these beyond the name. They have four companies.

4. For bridge building battalions, *see* Sec. **4**, para. 2.
For railway bridge building battalions, *see* Sec. **7**, para. 3.
For fortress construction battalions, *see* Sec. **8**, para. 2.
For ferry construction battalions, *see* Sec. **11**, para. 3.

11. Siebel ferry units

1. Siebel ferries (Sec. **18,** para. 1) are primarily the concern of the navy. They are also used by the G.A.F. for anti-aircraft purposes, and considerable attention has lately been paid to their use by army units (often referred to generally as *S.F.-Einheiten*). Certain construction battalions are specially trained in the assembly of these ferries, and may also provide crews.

2. These units come under Inspectorate 5 (Engineers) as regards the manning of the ferries, and under the Inspectorate of Fortresses as regards their assembly. Training is carried out by an engineer regimental staff at Lindau on Lake Constance ; training on the open sea by a training detachment (*Hochsee Lehrkommando*) at Terneuzen in Holland. Technical questions and the provision of the actual ferries are the responsibility of a special ferry command at Rotterdam.

3. *Ferry construction battalions* have their second-line transport (*Baukolonne*) strengthened, and may have a 5th company (*Pionierbaukompanie*) to provide the crews. This last is a combatant unit with 9 L.M.G., and is evidently designed for combined operations. Several battalions exist, but it is not known how many have a fifth company. The ferries are of course used for other purposes than combined operations, e.g. for transport, and for loading and unloading ships. Mention has been made of an equipment called the *engineer landing bridge*, used by these battalions for loading and unloading, but full details are not available.

4. *Engineer landing companies (Pionier-Landungskompanie).*—These companies have a strength of about 200 all ranks. Twelve landing boats (*L-Boot* : Sec. **18,** para. 2) are carried, with one M.G. each, and an unknown number of assault boats.

PART II. EQUIPMENT.

12. Bridging Equipment.

1. *Assault boats (Sturmboot).*—These are light wooden keelless boats, which will take seven men in addition to the crew of two. They are used in the initial stages of an assault crossing, and are powered by a separate unit--a 12 h.p. 4-cylinder water-cooled engine which drives a screw through a 13 ft. shaft contained in a tubular housing. Four men are required to carry the propulsion unit, and eight for the boats, which can be nested in threes on special trailers for transport. The speed of the boat when loaded is probably not more than 15 knots.

2. *Pneumatic boats.*—These boats are used in the second stage of an assault crossing. They are made of rubberized fabric in the form of an elongated ring, bulkheaded off into several chambers so that the boat cannot easily be sunk, and provided with a floor of wooden slats. They can be used for ferrying, or for rafting and bridging, when they are fitted with various types of light wooden superstructure. They are made in the following two sizes :—

    (a) *Small boat (kleiner Flosssack).*—This measures approximately 10 ft. by 4 ft. and will carry one passenger in addition to the crew of two. It takes about 5 minutes to inflate, weighs 110 lb., and rolls up into a cylinder 5 ft. long by 2 ft. diameter. It is not commonly used for rafting, but can be fitted either with a duckboard type of wooden superstructure to form a light infantry assault bridge (*Flosssack-Schnellsteg*), or with a double-tracked superstructure to form a bridge capable of taking motor-cycle combinations and light cars (*Kradschützensteg*).

    (b) *Large boat (grosser Flosssack).*—This measures approximately 18 ft. by 6 ft. and will carry one rifle or machine gun section in addition to the crew of seven. It takes 15 minutes to inflate, weighs 330 lb., and rolls up into a cylinder 7 ft. long by 3 ft. diameter. Boats can be joined either in pairs or in two pairs each in tandem, to form 2 and 4-ton rafts respectively ; alternatively a 4-ton raft with double tracked superstructure can be built. These rafts can be coupled together to form bridges, the exact rating of which is not known.

3. *Pontoon and trestle equipment.*—In addition to their own standard equipment, the Germans make considerable

use of former Austrian and Czech equipment. German equipment is of two main types :—

(a) *B pontoon and trestle equipment (Brückengerät B)*.—This is now the standard pontoon bridge in infantry and motorized divisions. It consists of superstructure of normal type, comprising roadbearers, chesses, and ribands, supported on undecked steel pontoons which can be used singly or joined together stern to stern to form pontoon piers. Three types of bridge can be built—4, 9, and 18-tons. The 18-ton bridge has recently been strengthened to an official rating of 20 tons by the introduction of a new type of trestle and by other methods details of which are not known. The actual capacity of the 18-ton bridge is unknown, but it will certainly take the Pz. Kw. IV tank (23 tons), and its maximum load is probably in the neighbourhood of 26 tons.

For assisting bridging operations motor boats are provided. These carry a 100 h.p. 6-cylinder water-cooled petrol engine and have a capacity of six men.

(b) *C pontoon and trestle equipment (Brückengerät C)*.—This appears to be an earlier type than the B, which may have been modelled on it and is now replacing it. Pontoons are similar in design to the B type, but smaller and of wooden construction, while superstructure is in made-up lengths measuring approximately 23 ft. × 2 ft. Four types of bridge can be built—an assault bridge, of single strips of superstructure supported on single pontoons, a 1-ton bridge consisting of a five-strip wide superstructure supported on double-pontoon piers, a 4-ton bridge similar to the 1-ton, but with twice the number of piers, and a 5·3-ton bridge, specially designed to take the 5·3-ton six-wheeled armoured car, in which each floating bay is supported on three piers.

4. *Box girder equipment.*—Two types of light box girder bridge are used by the Germans, the K and the D. Both may be used with pontoons and trestles to form multi-span bridges, and should therefore be classed as pontoon bridges with box girder type superstructure.

(a) *K equipment (Brückengerät K)*.—This is the standard bridge carried by engineers in the armoured division. The pontoons are of three-section type, and the superstructure is thought to have been modelled on the British small box girder bridge, Mark II; the principal members are similar and the launching nose identical. Bridges of two, three, and four girders caǹ be built, the full girder of 60 ft. being normally used. The capacities of these bridges are not definitely known, as the Germans are very conservative in their official ratings ; the two-girder bridge is said to carry 8 tons and the three-girder bridge 16 tons, while the four-girder, although its official rating is 16 tons only, will almost certainly carry 24 tons and probably more.

(b) *D equipment (Brückengerät D)*.—This equipment is used by mechanized pioneer platoons, and will take loads up to 9 tons. It is of the pontoon, trestle, and girder type ; no details are available, but the girder appears to be 30 ft. in length and to be composed of a central box section with two hornbeams.

5. *Semi-permanent heavy bridges*

(a) *L.Z. bridge*.—This is a through type sectional girder bridge which can be used for spans up to 145 ft. ; it will carry wheeled vehicles up to 18 tons and tracked vehicles up to 30 tons. One railway engineer company (Sec. 7, para. 2) can assemble and launch a 145 ft. bridge in 12–15 hours.

(b) *S equipment (Brückengerät S)*.—This is a heavy pontoon bridge (*schwere Schiffbrücke*) which is used only for heavy traffic across wide rivers. Its construction must be regarded as a major engineering operation. The pontoons are sectional, and the roadway, which is 16 ft. 6 in. in width, will accommodate two lines of traffic. Wheeled vehicles up to 24 tons and tracked vehicles up to 30 tons can be accommodated ; these figures must be reduced to 16 tons if two-way traffic is employed.

(c) *Herbert bridge*.—This is a heavy pontoon bridge with a built-up girder superstructure, and formed part of the equipment of the former Czechoslovakian army. It will take 20-ton wheeled and 24-ton tracked vehicles over a maximum unsupported span of 82 ft. The pontoons are of steel or light alloy, decked, and divided into eight or nine sections ; the superstructure is built up of pyramidal sections, from the apices of which transoms are suspended by means of special stirrups, these transoms carrying the roadway.

(d) *Railway bridges.*—Four types of railway bridges are known—the *Roth Wagner, Krupp, Kohn,* and *Ungarn*. As far as is known, none of these is of recent development, the *Roth Wagner* having been in use since the war of 1914–18. All are believed to be of the unit construction type, and to be built of standard parts which can be used alike in spans and piers.

6. *Improvised bridges.*—Great emphasis is laid in the German army on the construction of improvised bridges (*Behelfsbrücken*), and all engineer companies carry a small supply of timber for this purpose. Bridges vary from light timber footbridges (*Stege*) of various types, to semi-permanent bridges with a capacity of more than 20 tons. Apart from the lightest types, bridges are classified as of 2, 4, 8, 16, and 24-ton capacity, the last three being regarded as heavy bridges ; these bridges can be constructed on fixed or floating supports.

7. *Portable tank bridges.*—The only bridge of this type known is the " *Unger,*" a double track bridge 22 ft. in length, of timber construction, mounted on wheels, and said to be capable of carrying loads up to 22 tons.

13. Electrical and mechanical equipment

1. *Compressors and power tools.*—Of the two sizes of compressors carried by German engineers we have no details of the smaller (*kleiner Drucklufterzeuger* 34). The larger (*grosser Drucklufterzeuger* 34) is mounted on a trailer, has an overall weight of approximately 1,900 lb. and a capacity of 106 cu. ft. of air per minute, delivered at a pressure of 88 lb. per sq. in. Pneumatic tools driven by these compressors include drills, hammers, pile drivers, and probably small pumps. Power saws issued to engineer companies are normally petrol-driven, but there are reports that electrically-driven saws have also been used.

2. *Field generating sets.*—A large number of field generating sets, A.C. and D.C., ranging from 0·8 to 35 kilowatts, are in use in the German army, some being designed for special purposes.

14. Anti-tank and anti-personnel obstacles

1. *Concrete obstacles.*—These are of various types, and are the principal obstacles used in heavily fortified positions such as the Siegfried Line. " Dragons' teeth " are truncated pyramids up to 6 ft. in height, usually set out in from four to

eight parallel rows; concrete posts of various sizes and spacings are also used. Concrete cylinders similar to British types are employed in road blocks. Experiments have also been made with " stars," weighing about 350 lb., but it is thought that these have not proved very satisfactory.

2. *Steel obstacles.*—Rails and steel sections are employed to form barriers and road blocks; they are of varying heights and spaced at about 4 ft. centres. Another method of forming a road block is to support a rail horizontally across the road by massive concrete blocks at each end. The Belgian "Elements C," consisting of massive steel gates on rollers, 10 ft. in height and weighing 1½ tons, have been taken over by the Germans and are probably used on a considerable scale in Belgium and occupied France. Portable obstacles comprise various types of " tetrahedra " and " hedgehogs," the last-named consisting of three lengths of steel rails or girders joined together at right-angles at their centres. A type of curved steel rail obstacle, the object of which was to guide the nose of the tank upwards and thus force it into a vertical position, was used to reinforce the dragons' teeth of the Siegfried Line.

3. *Timber obstacles.*—The Germans recommend the use of the following :—

Wooden piles.

Felled trees, preferably sown with booby traps.

Log walls and ramps.

4. *Anti-tank ditches.*—The Germans lay down that anti-tank ditches should be 4 ft. 6 ins. to 6 ft. deep and 7 ft. 6 ins. to 21 ft. in width, with a 2 ft. 6 ins. earth parapet on each side, the vertical face reinforced where possible by a concrete wall or by normal revetment. Another type is the water ditch, the walls of which become soft and slippery when the ditch is filled with water. Stress is laid on the importance of camouflaging ditches, e.g. by coils of barbed wire laid in the ditch and covered with camouflage material; this method also serves to convert the ditch into an anti-personnel obstacle.

5. *Wire.*—All German engineer units are equipped with rolls of barbed wire (*S-Rolle*) and of plain wire (*K-Rolle*). The barbed wire can be used to form anti-personnel barriers of the single and double apron fence or concertina type, and can also be laid in rolls on roads forming anti-vehicle obstacles. Plain wire can be used in the same way to form anti-vehicle obstacles, usually in conjunction with anti-tank and anti-personnel mines.

15. Mines and mine detectors

1. *Anti-tank mines.*—The standard German anti-tank mine is the "*Tellermine*," which weighs 19 lb. and contains 11 lb. of T.N.T.; it is 12 ins. in diameter and 4 ins. high, with a convex top and flat bottom; a carrying handle is provided on one side. The ignition assembly is located in the centre of the lid and is operated by direct pressure; sockets are also provided in the side and base for attachment of pull-igniters and anchor wires, which form anti-lifting devices.

Tellermines are commonly laid 2–4 ins. below the surface; minefields may be laid in open spacing of one mine per yard of front or close spacing of two mines per yard of front. Certain guiding principles have been laid down regarding the layout of anti-tank minefields, but considerable variation has been encountered, and much has been left to the discretion of local commanders. It is common practice to protect fields of Tellermines with a row of anti-personnel mines, and in the Middle East mixed minefields consisting of alternate rows of Tellermines and Italian *B*.2 mines have been found.

Tellermines can also be laid on the surface to form hasty obstacles; for this purpose they may be connected by a special pressure bar (*Druckschiene*), about 5 ft. in length, which is used to join two or more mines together in "sticks" capable of being drawn rapidly across a road and forming a continuous obstacle which will detonate under pressure applied to any part of it.

A new type of anti-tank mine, known as the C.V.P.1, has recently made its appearance in the Middle East; it is of the same general design as the Tellermine but smaller, containing only 3½ lb. of H.E., and provided with an adjustable igniter by means of which the firing pressure can be varied and which also enables the mine to be fitted with a trip-wire for anti-personnel use.

A heavy box type mine containing 37 lb. of H.E. was identified on the Western Front in 1939–40 but has not made its appearance elsewhere; its use is thought to be confined to fixed defences.

The existence of a fourth type of anti-tank mine, the "*LPZ*," has recently been confirmed.

2. *Anti-personnel mines.*—The type generally issued to engineer units is the "*S-mine*" (*Schützenmine*). This is a cylindrical canister about 4 ins. in diameter by 6 ins. high containing 1 lb. of H.E. and about 350 steel balls packed round the filling. Initiation takes place by means of a push-igniter, a single pull-igniter and trip-wire, or two pull-igniters and wires attached to the mine by a Y-shaped adaptor. Mines can also be wired electrically for controlled firing. On

functioning, a propellent charge projects the mine into the air to a height of 2–3 ft. at which height it explodes, scattering the steel balls to a radius of 150–200 yards.

The standard layout for a field of these mines is a series of equilateral triangles with 15 ft. sides ; they are also laid in mixed minefields with Tellermines or as individual traps attached to road blocks and arranged to function when the obstacle is removed.

3. *Improvised mines.*—A great variety of improvised anti-tank and anti-personnel mines and booby-traps can be made up with standard demolition charges and push or pull-igniters.

4. *Mine detectors.*—German methods of detecting buried mines are of two kinds—mechanical and electro-magnetic. The mechanical method employs some sort of probe for locating the mine below the surface of the ground by actual contact ; the instrument normally used for this purpose is a tubular light alloy rod (*Minensuchstab*), with a hard steel point, which is said to give out a characteristic note on striking buried objects of metal, wood, or stone. Electro-magnetic methods of mine detection depend on the change in inductance of an oscillating circuit when placed near a conducting body ; in practice the circuit is embodied in a search coil mounted on the end of a rod of convenient length and moved over the surface of the ground, while the change of inductance is detected from variations in the note sounded in a pair of headphones worn by the operator. Several types of electro-magnetic detectors with different circuits are in use in the German army, and are commonly named after the town where they were originally produced, e.g., *Berlin, Köln, Frankfurt, Aachen.*

16. Demolition equipment

1. *Explosives.*—The standard explosive used is T.N.T. which the Germans initiate directly with a No. 8 or electric detonator, without using an intermediate primer. It is made up into the following prepared charges :—

100 gm. (3·5 oz.) cartridge (*Bohrpatrone* 28).
200 gm. (7 oz.) slab (*Sprengkörper* 28).
1 kg. (2·2 lb.) slab (*Sprengbüchse* 24).
3 kg. (6·6 lb.) slab (*geballte Ladung* 3 *kg.*).

The two smaller sizes are wrapped in waxed paper, the larger sizes being made up in zinc containers. All are provided with one or more threaded sockets for reception of detonators.

2. *Detonators.*—The latest type of No. 8 detonator for use with safety fuze is of aluminium, 2·4 in. long, 0·3 in. in diameter

and packed in wooden boxes of 15. A number of older commercial types, mainly of copper, are also in use. Detonators are normally contained in a brass or bakelite holder (*Zünderhalter*), which serves the double purpose of covering the junction of detonator and fuze, and of providing a thread for screwing into the charge.

The electric detonator (*Glühzünder* 28) is of the low tension hot wire type, and is contained in a holder similar to that used with the No. 8 detonator.

3. *Fuzes*.—German safety fuze (*Zeitzündschnur*) is similar to the British pattern and burns at a rate of approximately 2 ft. per minute, while the instantaneous fuze (*Knallzündschnur*) has a green gutta-percha covering, but in other respects is similar and can be handled in the same manner.

4. *Exploders*.—Several types of exploders for electrical firing of demolitions are in use. The latest pattern (*Glühzündapparat* 40) is a low tension exploder which will fire through an external resistance of 255 ohms.

5. *Igniters*.—The standard German igniter used for initiation of safety fuze is the *Zündschnuranzünder* 29 (*ZDSCHN ANZ* 29), which functions by withdrawal of a coiled wire through a match composition pellet. A later type (*ZDSCHN ANZ* 39) exists, but no details are known.

Other types are the push-igniter (*DZ* 35), the pull-igniter (*ZZ* 35), and the pull- and release-igniter (*Z. u.ZZ* 35). These all function by release of a spring-loaded striker on to a No. 8 detonator, and are largely used in the setting of improvised mines and booby-traps.

6. *Special assault demolition equipment*

(a) *Bangalore torpedoes* (*gestreckte Ladung*).—The standard type consists of 7 ft. lengths of steel tubing filled with H.E. and connected by bayonet joints. It is fired by a length of instantaneous fuze which runs along the whole length of the torpedo and is initiated by a No. 8 detonator. Torpedoes can also be improvised by securing grenade heads or standard H.E. slabs to boards or poles, and firing them in the same way as the standard torpedo.

(b) *Pole charge* (*geballte Ladung*).—This is used for attacking pillboxes and fortified positions, and consists of a number of standard explosive slabs fixed to the end of a pole. After a heavy bombardment and under cover of close supporting fire and smoke a man runs forward carrying the charge and places it on the sill of the embrasure; the charge is then fired either by a short length of safety fuze or electrically by an exploder operated by a second man.

(c) *Grenade charge.*—This consists of an ordinary stick grenade round the head of which are tied six other stick grenade heads. They are used against pillboxes in the same way as the pole charge, and also for attacking the tracks and turrets of A.F.Vs.

(d) " *Hollow* " *demolition charges* (*Hohlladung*).—These are conical H.E. charges designed to perforate cupolas and armour-plating in permanent fortifications. Three sizes, weighing 28, 30, and 110 lb., are in use. All are provided with a hemispherical hollow space on the side nearest the target, the effect of which is to concentrate the force of the explosion on a small surface area.

(e) " *Hollow ring* " *charges* (*Hohlringladung*).—These are designed for the destruction of gun barrels, and consist of pressed T.N.T. in thin anular metal containers, on the inner side of which is a small hollow space of semi-circular cross section. These charges are made in two sizes, containing $2\frac{1}{2}$ lb. and 7 lb. of T.N.T. respectively.

(f) *Mine-exploding net* (*Knallennetz*).—This is made of instantaneous fuze, and is used for clearing passages through minefields by detonating the mines. The net is made up in units 33 ft. long by 8 ft. broad, with a square 6 in. mesh, and is initiated by a length of safety fuze and a detonator, which can be fixed to any part of the net.

17. Flame throwers

1. In addition to the small and medium equipments, which have been in service use for some time, a recharging trolley and an improved pattern of small flame thrower are known.

2. *Small flame thrower.*—This is a one man load, although the crew normally consists of two ; the man carrying the weapon also fires it. The fuel oil is contained in a metal cylinder, which also holds the compressed nitrogen used as propellent. From a valve at the bottom of the cylinder the fuel oil passes through heavy armoured hose to the projector or gun. Ignition is by means of a ring of burning hydrogen gas surrounding the nozzle of the projector ; the hydrogen, obtained from a small cylinder carried together with the fuel container on the pack, is itself ignited by a low tension electric hotspot. The whole equipment is carried on the back.

3. *Medium flame thrower.*—The medium equipment is simply a larger edition of the small flame thrower and is carried on a two-wheeled trolley. The fuel content is greater,

but the range claimed for the weapon is the same as that of the small equipment.

4. *New type flame thrower.*—A new pattern of weapon has recently been examined which is a lightweight version of the small set (para. 2). The bulky containers of the latter have been modified and now take the form of two cylindrical section rings (like lifebuoys). The outer ring contains the fuel oil and the nitrogen, whilst the smaller inner ring is a hydrogen container. In all other respects this flame thrower is similar to the standard small model. There are indications that attempts are being made to produce large capacity pack flame throwers of lighter weight, and a variety of types and arrangements of fuel containers is to be expected.

5. *Recharging trolley.*—To assist servicing and maintenance in the field a recharging trolley is provided. This is an open cart mounted on two pneumatic tyred wheels and drawn by two men. The trolley carries fuel oil and a cylinder of nitrogen, both for replenishing the fuel container, charged hydrogen cylinders to replace those on the weapons, and spare parts for the small and medium equipments. Clamps are provided on the trolley for holding fuel containers in the proper positions during recharging. Total weight 680 lb.

6. Dimensions and performance of the various flame throwers are given in Table 11. It is to be noted that although total time of emission is given, it is normal for the flame throwers to be fired in a series of short bursts, each of 2–3 seconds duration.

TABLE 11

FLAME THROWERS

Detail	Small flame throwers	Medium flame throwers	New type small flame throwers
Weight (charged)	79 lbs.	225 lbs.	47 lbs.
Quantity of fuel oil carried	2·2 galls.	6·6 galls.	1·5 galls.
Range	25 yds.	25–30 yds.	25 yds.
Duration of continuous discharge	10–12 secs.	25 secs.	8 secs.

18. Landing craft

1. *Siebel ferries.*—It appears that the ferries fall into three main types as follows :—
   i. Heavy ferries.
   ii. Light ferries.
   iii. Transport ferries.

The heavy ferries carry heavy and light A.A. guns on two steel pontoons connected together in parallel by means of a platform. The pontoons are built up from pre-fabricated steel sections and the whole structure measures 75 ft. (length of one pontoon) by 56 ft. wide. Each pontoon has a beam of 18 ft.

The light ferries are of smaller construction and appear to be more lightly armed. At the four corners of each platform is a box-like construction which is probably some form of steel shield for protection of the gun crew.

The transport ferries are of similar construction except that the deck space is arranged to carry cargo.

2. *Engineer landing craft (Pionier-Landungsboot).*—These craft are known to exist, but details are not available. Present information points to one type having dimensions approximating 90 ft. by 4 ft. beam and the other 35 ft. by 10 ft. beam.

APPENDIX 1

ASSAULT DETACHMENTS

1. Assault detachments (*Stosstrupps*) are not permanent bodies with a fixed organization, but are formed from infantry and engineer units as required for particular operations. They vary greatly in size and in complexity. A detachment may be organized by a company to assist in gaining a company objective ; for more elaborate operations (e.g. for the intended attack on Tobruk, prevented by the British offensive of November, 1941), more elaborate detachments may be chosen and trained by battalions to take part in a concerted attack on a large prepared position. It appears however that all infantry and engineer units receive some general instruction on the work of assault detachments, and that the construction of these detachments follows fairly regularly the lines given in paras. 2–4.

2. Assault detachments of any size normally include the following :—

   (*a*) A party of engineers or infantry pioneers, with wire-cutters, bangalore torpedoes, etc., to clear away wire and other obstacles.

(b) A party of engineers and infantry, with flame throwers, pole charges, grenades, etc., for attacking pillboxes.

(c) A smoke party armed with smoke grenades and generators.

(d) An infantry support party, with M.Gs., mortars, anti-tank rifles, etc.

3. Where required, the following will be added :—

(a) A party of infantry, or, if necessary, engineers, with simple materials for making improvised bridges over anti-tank ditches, etc.

(b) A party of engineers with mine-detecting apparatus and spades.

(c) A wireless party with a pack wireless set.

4. Where the operation involves several stages, it may be necessary to add a supply party to carry up extra equipment etc., for the later stages of the attack.

APPENDIX 2

SPIGOT MORTARS

1. The German 20 cm. (7·9-in.) spigot mortar (*leichter Ladungswerfer* 40) is an engineer weapon, intended for use against minefields, wire, anti-tank obstacles, and weapon emplacements. Its present allocation is not known, but it is certainly not yet issued to divisional engineers.

2. The mortar is of normal spigot design, though, contrary to British practice, fixed ammunition is not used, the propellant case being attached to the top of the spigot before the bomb is loaded. The total weight of the mortar is 205 lb.

Two types of bomb are used, 46-lb. H.E. bomb with a 15-lb. T.N.T. filling for use against obstacles, and a smoke bomb of which no details are available. Reference has also been made to " harpoon ammunition " (*Harpunengeschoss*) This is to be used to draw prepared charges or mine-exploding net (Sec. **16,** para. 6 (*f*)) over wire or minefields, which cannot be approached in the normal way.

www.ingramcontent.com/pod-product-compliance
Lightning Source LLC
LaVergne TN
LVHW091309080426
835510LV00007B/434